Buddhism for Meat Eaters

Simple wisdom for a kinder world

Buddhism for Meat Eaters

Simple wisdom for a kinder world

JOSEPHINE MOON

SIMON &
SCHUSTER

BUDDHISM FOR MEAT EATERS:
SIMPLE WISDOM FOR A KINDER WORLD
First published in Australia in 2019 by
Simon & Schuster (Australia) Pty Limited
Suite 19A, Level 1, Building C, 450 Miller Street, Cammeray, NSW 2062

10 9 8 7 6 5 4 3 2 1

A CBS Company
Sydney New York London Toronto New Delhi
Visit our website at www.simonandschuster.com.au

ISBN: 978 1 76085 116 3

 A catalogue record for this
book is available from the
National Library of Australia

Cover design by Lisa White
Cover images adapted from Shutterstock and Creative Market
Typeset by Midland Typesetters, Australia
Printed and bound in Australia by Griffin Press

 The paper this book is printed on is certified
against the Forest Stewardship Council®
Standards. Griffin Press holds FSC chain
of custody certification SGS-COC-005088.
FSC promotes environmentally responsible,
socially beneficial and economically viable
management of the world's forests.

Contents

Why I Am Writing This Book

Of all the conversations I will have to have with my child – about topics like sex, drugs, death, dying, rejection or terrorism – what I dread the most is the one where I have to explain that meat comes from animals. We love animals but, yes, we eat them.

There can be a lot of shame involved with being someone who truly loves animals yet still eats meat. I don't see a lot of writing out there from animal-loving meat eaters, and I think shame is possibly a silencing force. Surely, if we really loved animals as much as we say we do, and if we really understood all the awful things that meat production does to the environment, then we would just stop eating meat, wouldn't we?

But what happens if we try and try but fail and fail?

From birth, I've had difficulty digesting foods and especially proteins. My body has never been an 'easy' one. I was iron deficient as a baby, too sleepy to eat, and given supplements. (I still have problems with iron, no matter how many supplements I take, and now have intravenous top-ups.) Baby formula wasn't right for me and so I refused to eat. My mother describes this as a terrifying time, one in which I grew thin and pale and was hospitalised for two weeks, where I was sedated and force-fed. Eventually, I was diagnosed with cow's milk protein intolerance and put onto goat's milk.

From age five, I began to tear ligaments in my ankle. From ten, I had terrible pain in my back that kept me from sleeping. At fifteen, sudden and severe sciatica struck, the cause of which no one could determine; a surgeon was consulted and there was a suggestion of cutting the sciatic nerve, which thankfully didn't eventuate. I am now certain that was the very start of what was, twenty-five years later, diagnosed as ankylosing spondylitis (an autoimmune disease that attacks the spine). Through my twenties and thirties, I was variously diagnosed with no less than twelve different conditions, including chronic fatigue syndrome – none of them life-threatening but all of them enough to make things challenging.

From thirteen, I began to try in earnest to become vegetarian and continued in one form or another for almost twenty-five years, without success. It was never a matter of lack of willpower or ignorance to animal rights issues (trust me, I wish I had *far* less knowledge of the horrors) or a particular love of the taste of flesh, it was a simple yet frustratingly complicated misalignment between spirit and body. Vegetable protein alternatives – chickpeas, soy, lentils, most seeds and nuts, quinoa, many types of beans, almost all grains, amaranth, buckwheat, mushrooms – give me varying combinations of indigestion, reflux, headaches, eczema, joint pain and abdominal pain. My mind is willing, but my body is not. (As an aside, a lot of animal proteins have the same effect on me too, but there are a handful I can tolerate.)

As a meat eater who adores animals, I have found this a difficult place to be. So much literature defends meat eating or veganism in this polarising, angry debate, in the same way the breastfeeding versus formula-feeding of babies is headlined in the media specifically to generate ugly discourse. Ultimately, I'm not sure how helpful this approach is.

For example, I was so convinced I would be breastfeeding my baby that I didn't even buy bottles while I was pregnant. I had bought into the literature that said 'breast is best' (and obviously if you *really* cared about your child then that was what you'd do, right?). Choice. That's what I thought it was – you could choose to either breastfeed *or* formula feed. Never once did I read a story explaining that sometimes the choice is simply taken away from you. My baby and I left the hospital on the bottle and I was devastated because I was completely unprepared for this eventuality.

Likewise, I see the same kinds of discussions about vegetarian diets. It's presented as a choice, a lifestyle you could simply opt into if only you cared enough.

For many people, it is. If you are a thriving vegetarian or vegan reading this book, I am deliriously happy for you. You're living my dream. But I know I'm not alone in having a body that seems to need a certain amount of meat in order to function at its best and it's taken me a long time to reconcile that, and longer still to be able to say it out loud.

From as far back as I can remember, I've had an intensely strong connection to animals. I have always seen them as just like people but in different bodies. I wanted to be a vet through my childhood until I hit Year 11 Physics, and it was blindingly clear that Physics and I were never going to get along. Without Physics, I wouldn't be able to apply for the veterinary science university course. (Never mind that I was killing it in Biology, a life science you would think was far more compatible with veterinary studies than abstract maths, but there you go. I also now know that I could never have been a vet and dealt with the surgeries, euthanasia and animal cruelty they have to confront.)

I studied journalism and then completed a postgraduate degree in education, becoming a high school teacher, while still aiming for a career as a writer. I changed jobs many times and took up a second career as a corporate editor. I started an environmental committee while working at an international engineering firm. I studied natural medicine and turned my hand to working with animals in this field. I ran workshops teaching people how to help their animals with massage, nutrition, vibrational essences, energy healing and communication. In my spare time, I fundraised for animal charities. Then I started a horse rescue charity and ran that for three years up until my son was born and I was simultaneously offered my first contract for a novel, launching my new career as an author. Serving animals – whether my own animals at home, or through the charity, or through raising money for other animal charities, or donating to animal charities, or through healing modalities, or the scores of animals I've picked up off the sides of roads – has always been 'my thing'.

Knowing and loving animals as I do, I *want* to be vegetarian. It's a great irony to me that I simply can't be. A variety of doctors and naturopaths have told me this over the years, as well as my own body, which suffers pain, dizziness and fatigue every time I cut animal protein from my diet. I cannot digest enough of the vegetarian proteins, regardless of what I do with them – long soak them, long boil them, slow cook them, ferment them, sprout them, grind them, combine them, powder them, or take digestive enzymes with them. Problem after problem arises. The dietary intolerances I was born with simply multiplied over the years along with autoimmune conditions (and yes, I've tried all the gut-healing remedies – and still use them – and spent veritable house deposits on alternative therapies and 'natural' doctors who promised to heal me, without success). I've had to work hard to make peace with my body and find the best way to keep it functioning at optimal levels. It's not that I don't eat vegetarian food; I just can't make it my primary source of protein. The reality is that this is the body I've been given in this lifetime. I can't fight against it, not if I want to be an active member of society. I want to be of service; for that, I need a body that is capable of doing so.

Understanding this, finally, I began to ask myself more interesting questions. If I was born into a body that couldn't cope with a non-animal diet, but my spirit really wanted it to, then this offered me an important journey of self-discovery (as well as years of frustration, guilt and turmoil). I started keeping a journal of my vegetarian wannabe woes to try to make sense of what was going on. Why was this conflict inside me? How could I reconcile it? I wrote and wrote and wrote until, eventually, I got my answer.

I had no idea.

With a heavy, grieving heart, I put that journal away and tried to tuck my guilty pain into places I didn't have to look at it. Until one day, I began to find freedom from my dilemma, and I found it in the most unexpected place: Buddhism. Yes, that great philosophy of compassion, with its number-one precept being 'do not kill', actually set me free.

What? Aren't all Buddhists vegetarians?

If like me you are a wannabe vegetarian, or perhaps a vegetarian who has recently found the need to temporarily eat meat (during pregnancy, for example), or find yourself hiding in the closet of shame in a room full of vegans because you love animals so much, then stay with me. There's hope for you too.

One

What I Love
About Buddhism

I first came across Buddhism when I was fourteen, in Year 9 at St Benedict's College, a Catholic girls' school in Brisbane. We were reading about it in a history class and I can vividly recall sitting at my desk, staring at the pages of the open textbook, my heart beating with excitement. While both sides of my family's backgrounds were Catholic and I'd been taught about Jesus and his teachings, my mother had branched out into New Age philosophies and she'd taught me about rebirth, past lives and karma. I knew I couldn't talk about those things with my peers or, indeed, the nuns, so I never really felt like my spirituality fit neatly into either Catholicism or the New Age. In the pages of that history textbook, however, I found a simplicity of truth – kindness, compassion, service, meditation and non-violence – that resonated with me, an overwhelming feeling of *I'm home*. Buddhism seemed to bring together my Catholic and New Age instruction, and then added even more layers of wisdom. It was practical. It was relevant. It was less a feeling of finding Buddhism as much as it was one of rediscovering it, the sense that I should have been Buddhist all along. It was such a *relief*.

'That's it. I want to be a Buddhist!' I declared to my mum that afternoon.

She nodded in support. 'Yes, I can see that would be good for you.'

Despite this, it would take me many more years to start accessing Buddhist experiences. These were the days before the internet, so it wasn't like I could simply research and learn online. Our school library was, unsurprisingly, not full of Buddhist scripture or teachings. There might have been a Christian church in every suburb, but that wasn't the case for Buddhist monasteries or temples. Brisbane in 1990 didn't have the level of multiculturalism that Sydney or Melbourne had. It would have been an exceptionally radical thing to declare to my Catholic teachers, school and friends that I was now a Buddhist. In short, I had no guidance and no real ability to independently seek it out.

In my mid-twenties, I started camping at the week-long Woodford Folk Festival north of Brisbane, a yearly festival of arts, music, cultures, the earth, new thinking and healing. The highlight of my time there every year was seeing the Tibetan Buddhist monks or nuns on site. I would sit in the hot, sweaty tents to listen to their chanting sessions and get up in the

3

dark to climb the hill for their New Year's Day dawn blessing for the coming year. I loved watching them walk through the festival in their maroon robes, slip-on shoes and shaved heads, their faces so serene, creating waves of peace just with their presence. I enjoyed observing them tap out their colourful sand mandalas – intricate artworks of balanced patterns and colours, representing the whole universe. The artworks were big pieces, ones in which these monastics sat down, cross-legged, bent over at the waist, their heads almost touching the floor, working on them for six days until complete.

I was always deeply moved by the dissolution cere-mony at the end, in which the entire masterpiece was swept away by a dry paint brush, gathered into a glass vase and poured into the lake. It was the concept of impermanence in action that affected me – art as a spiritual act and meditation process that exists in the making, not the keeping. It's a lesson I still try to hold at the forefront of my work as a writer, that the honour in what I do is in the creation of a story, not in the attachment to the publication or its (externally judged) 'success'. It's not an easy thing to do, especially when 'success' is attached to financial security and paying the mortgage, but I keep improving.

In 2008 I went to see a Buddhist Lama (a high-ranking monk) who travelled up from Victoria every now and then to offer healing sessions. I remember his beautiful, loving compassion as he lay his hands on me. I remember crying. I remember him telling me that it was very important that I stop being so hard on myself, to be gentle with myself, to love myself. To be compassionate with *myself*. I had by then been diagnosed with chronic fatigue syndrome and knew the truth in what he said because if there was one thing that condition had done for me it was to start breaking down my self-criticism and perfectionist tendencies. It had begun to teach me to let go of many things in my life – career goals, high expectations, a regular income, and a whole range of belief systems about healing and what I 'should' be doing – simply because I had to.

Over many years, I collected books on Buddhism. I saw His Holiness the Dalai Lama speak at Australia Zoo one year and felt nothing but love for him – for his lack of ego, his huge heart, the radiant glow that seemed to emanate from him. I wanted to be just like him. The moment Hubby and I achieved our dream of moving to the Sunshine Coast in 2012, I visited a local Buddhist centre, and now I regularly attend courses up there to continue my education.

Even though I wanted to be able to call myself a Buddhist, I never thought I could because, despite my best efforts, I couldn't give up eating meat. That belief changed at the beginning of 2018.

My golden retriever Daisy (and first 'baby') was one day seemingly perfectly healthy, eleven years old but still acting like a puppy, and the next day struck down by seizures that rolled on and on, just minutes apart. She spent two nights and two days in emergency, confounding the specialists who couldn't work out what was triggering these seizures in an otherwise healthy, young-looking dog, only to be finally diagnosed with multiple tumours in her liver and spleen, which were triggering her heart into massive arrhythmias and then seizures. I brought her home, expecting we'd have a bit of time to write out a bucket list and nurture her last days, but in the middle of the night wave after wave of seizures struck and went on for hours. The vet came to our house the next morning and we let her go, sitting in our garden where she so loved to dig.

It broke me. It was grief such as I'd never experienced before. I say that, acknowledging that I have been fortunate in life so far and have not lost my spouse, a parent, my sister or, God forbid, my child; but the day Daisy died I lost my best friend. The hole she left behind was enormous and I was floundering.

I turned back to Buddhism, reading everything I could get my hands on and attending seminars.

Then I started an online group to share knowledge and resources for raising families with a Buddhist mindset, and began to run monthly gatherings for those who could make it. It was Buddhism that pulled me through this difficult time. Along the way, and quite by accident, I discovered wisdom that also helped me with my decades-old issue of how to reconcile meat eating with my desire to be vegetarian. Buddhism was the gift that kept on giving.

While Buddhism becomes a religion for some people, it is first and foremost a philosophy and practice, and in that sense anyone can be a Buddhist and benefit from the practices regardless of their religious persuasion.

My experience of Buddhism is one of non-judgement. The path of the Buddhist is to relieve one's own suffering (from disturbing emotions) and regain mental equilibrium, and then by extension to alleviate others' suffering so that they may also regain equilibrium. Non-judgement applies to the self first, then to others.

Even when it comes to the law of karma – that what you do comes back to you, whether 'good' or 'bad' – which in Western society can be interpreted as something vengeful, Buddhists don't attach judgements to people's actions. You are responsible for your thoughts and actions and you *can* choose to do whatever you like. That's between you and your karma. Buddhism meets you wherever you're at, right now.

At its core, Buddhism says you already have everything inside you in order to be a peaceful, happy, loving human being. Isn't that beautiful? You're okay, right now! At the same time, it acknowledges that life is hard – forget the rainbow-coloured fairy dust, life *hurts* – and it gives you the tools you need in order to master your own emotions and experience of the world to relieve your suffering and find peace. It is flexible – it understands that life is quintessentially not black and white, and that wisdom is needed at every stage. It encourages you to question teachings, not to accept them at face value but to delve into them deeply until you are completely satisfied they are correct. If something doesn't resonate with you, you can leave it aside. The Buddhist community is not interested in converting you. They are the epitome of living by example. If you are attracted to what they teach and what they do, if their authenticity inspires you, you may naturally want to follow them. If not, so be it. A Buddhist knows that the only person they can change is themself and is therefore primarily concerned with developing their own peaceful mind and compassionate heart, not in changing others.

Buddhism gives you tools for life, tools for peace, tools for happiness. You're not required to pay any money, to make public commitments to being a

Buddhist, to leave your family or loved ones, to travel overseas, to give your power away, to fear death, or fear judgement, or to follow anything without question. You can start today, in your lounge room, in the doctor's office, on the train, or in your garden because you have the skills inside you to start walking the Buddhist path towards enlightenment.

For me, one of the most sensible, practical and compassionate philosophies of Buddhism is that of the Middle Way – finding moderation between extreme self-pleasure or extreme self-denial.

In this book, I will:

o look at the Buddhist wisdom I have gained that has helped me to reconcile a huge conflict in my life (that is, eating meat)

o share what I've learned in the hope it might help you too (that is, to help you alleviate your suffering)

- give you practical tools to help navigate these tricky waters
- offer points of reflection that you could explore in your own personal journal in discovering what works best for you.

In this book, I will not:

- in any way claim to be an expert (the Buddhist philosophy encourages us all to constantly view everyone and everything with 'beginner's eyes'; I am a student of Buddhism and always will be)
- make a case for eating meat (I'm not here to defend meat eating)
- make a case for veganism (I'm not here to convince you to take up a plant-based diet)
- traumatise you and tell you about the horrors of animal cruelty (I'm pretty sure you already know what they are and it's not the point of these discussions)

- try to convert you to Buddhism (remember, you don't have to identify as a Buddhist to benefit from the tools and wisdom).

So, let's start at the beginning with an overview of Buddhism.

Two

Buddhism on a Plate

Buddhism began in what is now modern-day Nepal over two-and-a-half thousand years ago. The person we know as the Buddha today was born into wealth and privilege as Prince Siddhartha Gautama, and he later left his family and sheltered life to go and experience the wider world. He encountered suffering for the first time – including sickness, old age and death – and this propelled him to find a way for humans to rise above suffering. At that time, the local people worshipped many gods, were tied into a caste system, and believed they had to pay money to their gods in order to keep them happy. If the gods were happy, they would be happy. Buddha thought differently, believing everyone already had everything they needed to be happy inside of them. He also believed that every person was equal, regardless of the situation of birth, which was a radical notion for his day.

During his time of discovery, Buddha experimented with fasting from food to see if this would bring him closer to enlightenment. He became so thin and weak that he almost died. From this experience, he came to the understanding of the Middle Way – the need for moderation. After six years of meditation and teaching, he achieved enlightenment and became a Buddha, continuing to travel and teach, gathering a significant following. Buddhists believe that anyone can become a Buddha – one who has reached freedom from all their mental suffering and instead lives from the states of positive virtues only – including you and

me, and there have been many famous ones throughout history. But generally, when people speak of
Buddha, they are referring to Prince Siddhartha, the
founder of what we now call Buddhism.

Buddha ate meat.

Does this shock you? It shocked me when I first
read that. But to appreciate why Buddha ate meat, we
would have to consider the time and place in which
he lived. As he was born into a wealthy family, his
diet would have included meat. Furthermore, in
his life as a monk, while seeking enlightenment, he
would have relied on alms-giving from locals for
his daily food, having no control over what he was
offered. Many monks in Asia still receive their daily
food through alms from locals, who place these
offerings into the monks' begging bowls. Monks
may be required to accept and eat whatever they are

given with gratitude – be that vegetables, rice, beef or grasshoppers.

But considering there are three main schools of Buddhism – Mahayana, Theravada and Vajrayana – and diversified branches of thought within those, you will find varying scriptures and rules about meat eating. The schools of South-East Asia tend to promote vegetarianism. Depending on what geographical location each school arose in, the rules may change, which is understandable. If you were a nomad in the high altitude and harsh conditions of Tibet, where fresh fruit and vegetables may only be available for short windows of time, then you wouldn't survive if you didn't eat meat. For me, this is a key point when we're grappling with our emotions around eating meat. This is the embodiment of the Middle Way, avoiding extremes when you have a need to do something to keep yourself well.

It is said that in some sutras (scriptures), Buddha gave very specific instructions for when it was okay to eat meat. He said that in order to do so, the consumer must not have seen the animal killed, must not have heard the cries of the animal as it was killed, and must not have suspected the animal was killed for oneself.

I find this interesting. During my years of trying to work out what side of an imagined ethical line I stood on, I once tried to talk myself into being responsible enough to know where my meat came from. In 2006, I came across a farmer who raised grass-fed cattle with no hormones or antibiotics, butchered her own animals and delivered the meat to your door for half the price of certified organic meat. I decided this was a tremendously ethical way of consuming meat, with far less stress to the animal, better outcomes for boutique farmers, supporting local industry, low food miles and so on. In theory, I believed that the best way to eat meat must surely be to raise your own animal with love and care and then give thanks for its life at the end, taking inspiration from some cultures around the world who hunt as necessary and pray for the animal's spirit. But I knew I'd never be able to do that, so buying direct from the farmer seemed like the next best thing; however, it didn't go well for me emotionally.

My journal from the time describes my experience.

When I rang to enquire, Becky told me that we could buy half a side or a quarter of a side of meat and it would be cut up any way we wanted. I was taken aback. I struggled to think about a 'quarter of a side'. That was a quarter of a cow. She was going to kill a cow for me! I spoke to Hubby about it, cried and fretted. Logically, I knew it was no different than going to the butcher, but it felt so much more personal. I felt my hand was signing the execution slip.

And I felt like such a hypocrite.

Becky questioned me about how we wanted the meat. She spoke in anatomical terms and I didn't even know what they meant. What did we want done with the rib roast? The blade? The rounds and rump? How thick did we want our steaks?

I told her we didn't really eat steak and she did little to hide her gasp of shock. She couldn't understand me. I explained that we really only ate stir-fry strips and a bit of mince.

Did we want bones and offal? I agreed to take these to give to the dogs.

The offal was disgusting. It made me retch to see pieces of tongue, blue and bumpy, just sliced out of a cow's mouth. The heart. The bean-shaped kidneys and enormous liver pieces. The dogs thought they were disgusting too and refused to eat them.

The meat came in two huge boxes and I had to separate it all into bags, pulling it out of the blood-filled plate before freezing. I tried to think happy thoughts, not wishing to contaminate the meat with my energy; I tried to give thanks and blessings to the cow; I tried to think of all the environmental and health benefits *of eating meat this way. It took us months to finish the meat. Becky was shocked it took us so long to finish it and was horrified when I explained that the dogs ended up eating most of the T-bone steaks for dinners. The whole experience was excruciating.*

We gave up eating beef for a long time after that.

Of course, it would be easy at this point for pro-vegetarian people to say that this experience shows me that it's wrong to eat meat, that clearly, this was my spirit – my moral compass – telling me that eating animals is wrong. Remember, though, my spirit doesn't necessarily disagree with this. It's my body that has the meat-eating need here, not my moral compass, hence the internal conflict and the reason for writing this book.

While logically, I can appreciate the argument that there is no difference to eating meat you've bought from a butcher or ordering the killing of the animal to then eat the meat, all I can say is that whole experience felt ghastly.

I'm simply saying I find it *interesting* that Buddha made that distinction too.

In those teachings, the act of eating meat itself is considered karmically neutral – an action that is neither 'good' nor 'bad'. It is akin to scavenging, not killing. Of course, it gets more complicated than that because some schools of Buddhism claim Buddha left direct instructions not to eat meat. Buddha himself never wrote down his instructions, his assistants did, much as Jesus never wrote the gospels, his disciples did. Consequently, vegetarianism and meat-eating can be a hotly contested topic within the differing schools of Buddhism.

It may also surprise you to know that His Holiness the Dalai Lama, a tremendously loved figurehead in Buddhism, well-known to the people of the West, actually eats meat. When I heard him speak at Australia Zoo in 2007, he gave a long discussion on

23

compassion for animals (he is particularly passion-ate about chickens) and promotes vegetarianism as a great thing to do if you can manage it. But he developed a health condition and became very sick and the result was that his doctors advised him to include at least some meat into his diet in order to stay well and so that is what he does.

Hang on a minute . . . did the Dalai Lama just give me permission to eat meat?

The full impact of his admission didn't really hit me until a decade later, when I suddenly integrated that with my own experience. The Dalai Lama had reconciled his need to eat at least some meat to stay healthy with his compassion for all sentient beings. It was the Middle Way in action. Maybe I could do it too.

It makes a lot of sense that if you live in an area that has a yearlong bounty of vegetarian supplies (that is, not the mountain tops of Tibet), and you have a desire to not eat meat, and you and your body are aligned

24

to do so, then adopting a vegetarian lifestyle is clearly a great thing to do. This is why here in the West we might be mistaken for thinking that all Buddhists are vegetarian. In many ways, a vegetarian or vegan lifestyle could be considered a privilege, as not everyone has easy access to fancy vegan cheeses, milks and ice-cream, chia seeds (which come from South America, so the food miles for the rest of us are pretty wild), pre-packaged seaweed and hemp products, coconut products, nut meats, quinoa and chickpea pasta and so on. It's clearly much easier when you can pluck these things from the shelf than if you are living in remote, rural or impoverished situations where you don't have easy access to all the foods you need to have a fully formed nutritious diet. Whichever side of the Buddhist vegetarian line you might find yourself on, it's worth considering that the fact that there *is* still so much conjecture within Buddhist circles across the globe about whether or not one must be vegetarian speaks strongly to the realisation that there simply is no black and white rule and each person must consider their own unique needs at any given time.

The Four Noble Truths

At the core of Buddhist philosophy are the Four Noble Truths. These are translated in varying forms but my simplified understanding of them is this:

1. Suffering exists, everywhere and for everyone.
2. Attachment is the cause of suffering.
3. There is a way to end suffering.
4. The way to end suffering can be found in the teachings of The Eightfold Path. (In simplistic terms, these are: Right Understanding, Right Intention, Right Speech, Right Action, Right Livelihood, Right Effort, Right Mindfulness and Right Concentration.)

The first of the four Noble Truths of Buddhism states that suffering exists. We know it, right? We feel it, we see it, we experience it, we cause it. The second of the Truths is where it gets tricky. This truth says that attachment is the root cause of suffering. 'Attachment' can also be described as grasping, straining, clutching or fixation. Attachment relates to anything – objects, fantasies, people, houses, careers, self-identity and ideals. Rigid thinking leads to unhappiness. Perhaps, then, if we let go of our fixed belief in one thing or another and adopt a more flexible, gentle attitude we can see that what we need can change minute by minute. Instead of attaching a label to ourselves as vegan, or vegetarian, or meat eater, or flexitarian or pescatarian or any other variation, we could just *be* a person making the best possible choice in any given moment.

The Middle Way

The Middle Way must be decided upon by each person. What is *your* middle way? It might take you some experimentation to find out. It took me many years to find the Middle Way with my health support networks. At one point, I avoided any medications or medical doctors, fiercely believing that there was a natural medicine answer for everything. It cost me significant amounts of money to follow this path and I wasn't much better off for it. After spending more than two years trying to avoid ankle surgery by any other means possible, I finally connected with a great surgeon who was perfect for me. It was a huge lesson and turning point, and since then I have walked the middle path between pharmaceutical medicine and natural medicine. I now truly accept that all types of treatment are here for good reason and different approaches are needed at different times. These days, I rely on research, logical reasoning and a good dose of intuition to lead me in the right direction.

There are many examples like this in our life, which may apply to alcohol and sugar consumption, our spending habits, our relationships with others or our work environments. Learning to work with the Middle Way in one area of life might help us to apply the same principles to other areas of our life. For some people, vegetarianism is the Middle Way, having found they didn't thrive on a vegan diet, and adding eggs and dairy back into their life. For some people, including some meat or fish in their diet is the Middle Way. Only *you* can decide what your middle way is, regardless of what other people try to tell you it should be.

Journal Questions

1. What examples of the Middle Way do you see in practice in your life right now? (Consider areas such as health, diet, finances, relationships, entertainment, work, friendships or spirituality.)

2. Are there areas of your life where you could pull things back to get closer to the Middle Way? Likewise, are there areas where you could relax ideals to get closer to the Middle Way?

3. How does it make you feel to learn that Buddha ate meat and gave instructions for meat eating?

4. Are you able to identify attachments in your attitudes to food that might be causing you suffering?

Three

Non-violence:
I'm on the spectrum
and so are you

At the heart of a Buddhist practice is the idea of leading a life of non-violence, both in action and in thought. At first, it seems a straightforward and obvious notion – do not kill, do not hit, do not yell, do not hate, and so on. Veganism, then, seems like a significant contribution to this commitment, and of course it is. But when you look deeper, a life of non-violence is not as easy as it seems.

The majority of our food is, regrettably, still grown using pesticides and herbicides, both of which kill millions of grasshoppers, caterpillars, moths, insects and, alarmingly, bees. The seriousness of the impact of these chemicals on bees is such that more than a dozen European Union countries have begun banning popular chemicals that could be the cause of the destruction of our bee populations. It is estimated that a third of our global food crops and up to ninety per cent of flowering plants and trees, such as those found in our native forests, are reliant on bee pollination. A world without bees is not a world I want to live in. Arguably, advocating for bee safety should be at the top of all of our priorities.

From a Buddhist perspective, the life of a bee is just as valuable as a dog, cow or human; there is no discrimination. I think this is a sensible conclusion because any time we try to assign more 'value' to one life over any other we are inviting a slippery slope to condoned cruelty (and only a hop, skip and jump to the same judgements on human diversity).

Suffering exists everywhere and a vegetarian diet isn't free of violence and death. Aside from the chemicals used in farming, digging in the earth and ploughing fields also kills multitudes of worms, beetles and insects. If we accept that no animal's life is more valuable than any other, then we accept that a plant-based diet leaves us with blood on our hands also.

I've heard vegans argue that being vegetarian isn't anywhere near good enough. Most of us would be well aware of the horrors endured by mother cows and their baby boy cows, otherwise known as bobby calves. (Don't worry, I'm not going to traumatise you here. You can do an online search about this if you want to know more.) Eating commercially produced dairy-based cheese and butter, ice-cream, chocolate, cream and milk contributes to extensive suffering. Likewise, the production of eggs involves extreme cruelty in the chicken trade. Even if they are organic (which is the

33

only way to ensure they truly are 'free range', as this is a term not well monitored), the male chicks experience a violent death not long after hatching, and debeaking may still be done, as well as the eventual slaughter of the chicken when she is considered to be no longer productive.

Bees suffer again during honey production and commercial pollination ventures (of fruit and nuts, for example). Bee farmers may hire out their bees to farm crops each year. They wrap up their hives in plastic (and obviously some are killed or left behind during this process), put them on trucks and transport them vast distances to the farms. Some bees die from the stress. Some may die each time the beekeeper opens the hive and pulls out frames of honey as it's easy for them to get squashed. Then when they've finished their tour of duty on the farms, they are wrapped up and trucked away again, and more lives are lost in the process. Queen bees are deliberately bred and posted around the country in plastic tubes and when they are considered to be old (usually at one to two years of age, which is approximately half their lifespan in the wild), they are killed and a new queen is imported to the hive.

These realities bring us face-to-face with Buddha's First Noble Truth: that suffering exits, everywhere, all the time. The fact is that simply by being alive and walking in this world, we encounter suffering and we cause suffering. Just by living in a developed nation, we are benefiting off the backs of the developing nations that provide the majority of our goods. Those labourers are often underpaid, work long hours, having little or no protection from exploitation, perhaps in dangerous conditions, and sometimes even die (in factory fires, for example).

If you live in a house, more than likely the land your house rests on used to be covered in forest. But it was cleared to make way for your home, killing many types of animals, not to mention destroying trees and vegetation essential to our survival (oxygen and clean air). In Australia, our Indigenous populations have been displaced and all manner of atrocities enacted in order for us to take the land to live on. If you drive a car and use electricity, you are contributing to greenhouse gases and global warming, which is decimating the polar bear population (just for a start), because polar ice caps are melting, leaving them with less landmass to hunt for food. The more polar bears have to swim, the more exhausted they get, the less they can feed, the thinner they get, the more exhausted they get, and so on.

If you did an inventory of everything in your house, it would probably come as no surprise if almost all of it contains plastics or synthetics of some kind, which are polluting our planet in both landfill and waterways. Palm oil is everywhere, hiding in the most unlikely of places, such as in cosmetics, toiletries, soaps and foods. Palm oil, as I'm sure you know, is felling the forests of Borneo and is directly responsible for killing orangutans, which are on the brink of extinction.

Where does your toilet paper come from? Chances are, forests are cut down to create something for you to use for a second and flush away with precious rainwater. Pet food is a minefield (we'll revisit this in Chapter 9). And if you've ever taken any kind of medication, then you're ingesting medicine that has been tested on and experimented on animals.

It's all rather depressing.

But does this mean we should give up? No, of course not. The point of this little foray into darkness, perversely, is to encourage you to give yourself a break. If you're reading this book, I'm guessing it's because you struggle with conflicting emotions and guilt about various choices, including eating meat. You might have talked yourself into believing that you are a bad person, or a weak person, or a shameful person because you cannot do the thing you think you need to do.

Consider the Second Noble Truth: attachment is the cause of suffering. Are you causing yourself unnecessary suffering by clinging to an ideal version of yourself that (you perceive) you keep failing to meet? Come, now, there are enough people in the world ready to take you down for no good reason, don't do it for them.

I'm reminded here of my healing session with the visiting medicine Lama who told me, with great kindness, that I had to be more gentle with myself.

Consider too the violence of thoughts. Most of our self-talk is negative, condemning, shaming, harassing and agitating. If we're honest, a lot of our internal dialogue about other people is also negative. We are judging people all the time, for how they parent their kids, for what they look like, for what they're eating, for how they're driving, for how they do their work, for how committed or otherwise they are to their jobs and families. For a Buddhist, the primary goal in life is to develop a peaceful mind and compassionate heart. Everything else stems from that.

Buddhist wisdom encourages us to control our disturbing emotions. Disturbing emotions are any that pull us up very high or down very low, emotions that take us out of our centre, which is the only place from where we can control our wild 'monkey mind' (the mind that leaps to one thought, then another, then another – chatting, grasping, relentlessly swinging from one branch to the next). Here in the West, we tend to think that excitement is a good thing, as well as intense love, and that other emotions such as fear, anger or jealousy are 'negative' emotions. It is significant, I think, that Buddhism doesn't label heavy emotions as 'negative' emotions. But even in the case of 'positive' emotions, such as love, we humans have a tendency to twist this into something disturbing, such as possession, need and desperation – all forms of clinging attachment. The aim is always to be at the centre, the only space in which we can truly stay in the present moment and are able to make the best choice at any given time. This is not to say we can't have fun. On the contrary, the Buddhist monks and nuns I've met over the years have some of the best senses of humour I've ever encountered. They laugh a lot. When I heard His Holiness the Dalai Lama speak, I was in awe at how much he laughed, even while talking about difficult topics.

In my first year at university I was enrolled in a Bachelor of Science in Environmental Studies and I had a dream of being an ecologist (until I realised that statistics and I were never going to get along and I was really much more of a writer than a human calculator). I could be somewhat of a ranty advocate – for environmentalism, animal rights, solar power, refugees, human rights and pretty much any other social justice issue you could encounter. I was fuelled with anger about what was happening in the world and disgust for political leaders who abuse our planet, and I feared for the future. In their own way, these emotions were violent emotions. Don't get me wrong, I wasn't imagining or doing anything typically considered violent (like blowing things up or breaking and entering), but once you start seeing anyone else as an 'other', you've lost your centre, lost your humanity and tend towards judgement, blame and criticism, which are forms of violent thought. Did I get things done? Yes, I did. Did I alienate people along the way? Undoubtedly.

It can be a difficult line for all of us, regardless of what we're passionate about, to find a way to maintain compassionate action and a calm, clear mind that is free of disturbing emotions. As previously mentioned, one of the things I love about Buddhism is that it meets you wherever you are on the journey towards enlightenment and welcomes you to continue your practice of compassionate awareness and action. Full-on diatribes about the evils of eating meat, or deliberately trying to traumatise people on Facebook with horrifying images of cruelty, or dismissing someone as being 'not vegan enough', isn't meeting people where they are. It's deliberately inflicting violence of thought.

My journal reminds me that in 2010, I experienced some of my own behaviour of my youth coming back to me. (Karma in action, perhaps.) I refer to this incident as *The Meanest Vegan I've Ever Met*.

I decided I wanted to hold a vegetarian 'Christmas in July' at our property. I've always found Christmas tricky as I never eat pork, can't stand to be around shellfish while people peel them and crack open their claws, and don't much enjoy the sight of a big turkey carcass being picked over. So, the idea was to enjoy a warm celebration with my favourite vegetarian friends, a heap of yummy food, some mulled wine and a roaring fire with our cats and dogs wandering around inside, our horses and chickens wandering around outside, and with the neighbour's cows who liked to hang out at the fence. I prepared my menu, cleaned the house, bought the wine and prepared myself for a fun day with people I loved.

The day before the event, one of my guests messaged me to ask if she could bring an acquaintance of hers. He was a vegan and an activist, and they wanted to check out the slaughterhouse about forty-five minutes away from our place for the purpose of surveillance. After initial panic at my plans changing at the last minute, I added in vegan options, rearranged sleeping quarters and was back on my way.

The man arrived wearing an aggressive-looking black T-shirt with *Vegan Mafia* splashed across it in bloodlike red, immediately raving about the abattoir they'd stopped to visit. My very affectionate cat Bucket (short for 'Bucket of Love' because he is so cuddly), greeted him by rubbing his face on the man's leg. In response, this agitated and high-strung man *flicked* my cat's ear. 'I don't do cats,' he said, disgusted and flicked Bucket's ear again. I went rigid inside, tried not to overreact and locked Bucket up in a bedroom.

As the afternoon wore on, the man kept us in stunned silence as he raved about the stupidity of people and their crimes against animals and put most of the general populace down with arrogant intellectualising about their lack of brains or imagination. He also spent a lot of time 'tormenting' (that was his word) my dog Goldie, by roughly flapping her ears back and forth in a way that would have been disturbing to her. I could see her eyeing him warily, shuffling slightly from foot to foot, unsure what to do. I asked him to 'go gently' because she was 'a bit fragile' (Goldie had all manner of emotional and mental challenges), but he ignored me. I separated Goldie from him.

Wasn't this man supposed to love animals?

When we went outside for some air, he relentlessly teased my other dog, Daisy, who was completely obsessed with tennis balls, by 'fake throwing' the ball for her, and laughing nastily each time she got confused and tried to run after a ball that had never been thrown in the first place. I cracked a bit then and told him outright to 'stop teasing my dog' because that was a horrible thing to do to her. I really wanted him out of my house and out of contact with my animals. His actions towards them felt mean if not actually cruel. It was the last thing I'd expected of a vegan.

My journal notes that, at this point, I had a break-through.

Realisation: it's not about being vegetarian, it's about compassion. Being vegan doesn't make you a good person, a kind person, or a compassionate person. Being vegan just makes you a vegan.

Being a vegan didn't necessarily have anything to do with *love*. Love might have been my driving energy behind wanting to be vegan, but for other people it might have been any number of things, including an attachment to an ideology or a need to feel superior or even just a passing phase.

After meeting that man, I realised that the only thing that makes someone a good, kind and com-passionate person is *acting* like a good, kind and compassionate person. Clinging to an ideology (veganism, in this case) is just that – clinging. The cause of all suffering, as Buddha tells us, is attachment. This man's attachment to an idea without demonstrating any real loving action was certainly causing suffering to everyone around him that day, as well as to my animals and likely to himself. My attachment to believing that veganism would make me a better person and suddenly end all my contributions to suffering in the world had been causing me suffering too, because I hadn't managed to achieve it and constantly felt like a failure.

After he left my house, I collapsed into the lounge chair to snuggle my cat, feeling deflated. I felt my vegetarian Christmas had been ruined. I had been attached to an idea of a joyful, lovely event with friends that also happened to express my desire to do right in the world. I'd been looking forward to it for weeks and it imploded in a truly unpleasant way. My attachment to what I thought I wanted and needed caused me suffering when I didn't get what I'd wanted. I'd held pride (a disturbing emotion), wanting to prove to myself and others that I was striving to be a good person, as well as the need (attachment) to do something to ease my guilt and prove to my (judgemental) friends that I was 'just as good' a person as them. No wonder it all fell down! But I got something much deeper that day – a powerful lesson in what compassion really means and the wisdom to see that it didn't fit neatly into a definable box. Veganism was but one road on the entire map of compassion.

Journal Questions

1. What makes a person a 'good person'? How do you know?

2. Do you feel like you're a good person? Why? Or why not?

3. Have you ever felt the need to pretend, hide or strive towards veganism in order to gain someone else's approval? If so, what might it have been *in you* that led to those feelings?

4. List all the ways you demonstrate your compassion.

5. List all the ways you hold compassion in your heart.

6. Do you hold violent thoughts towards yourself? How might you be gentler with yourself?

7. What disturbing emotions do you encounter when you think about eating meat? Can you think of any ways to change these?

Four

Wisdom and Compassion:
To act or not to act,
that is the question

Wisdom and compassion go hand in hand. We've already looked at the ways in which compassionate action exists on a spectrum. Abstaining from eating meat is one potential act of compassion but is far from the only one. Our choices for compassionate action radiate in all directions and if, like me, you share your life with animals you will have to confront the balancing act of compassion and wisdom on a daily basis. I'd like to take some time here to consider several examples of the interplay between wisdom and compassion, because in doing so it shows us again and again just how complicated our human–animal relationships are. The balancing act we learn from in one arena we can apply to another, including that of meat eating. Furthermore, we see that a commitment to abstaining from meat doesn't absolve us from having to make difficult choices in other areas. Accepting this, I suggest that it is possible to 'fail' in one arena while 'excelling' in others, and that neither is a better arena in which to triumph. It's all part of the same spectrum.

Rescuing

You might have a boatload of compassion for animals, but if you don't use wisdom to balance this you are in danger of running off course. I saw this a lot in my time running a horse rescue. Compassion would say that rescuing a horse from a slaughter yard would be a wonderful thing to do. But wisdom would say that if you don't have the financial and practical ability to then look after and rehabilitate that horse, all you are doing is potentially bringing more suffering into your life and the horse's life.

Rescuing an animal off death row can give you an instant emotional high. You singlehandedly pulled this beautiful, sentient being out of the jaws of death and suffering! It's exhilarating. But then, reality sets in. Maybe you take the dog home to find that it bites your child on the first day. Maybe you take the horse home to find that it is terrified of people and you can't get near it to treat that huge open wound it has, you have no money to pay for specialised training to improve its ability to be handled, and you don't have time because that wound is septic. Maybe you rescue an echidna off the road that was clipped by a car and put it in your backseat to take to a wildlife carer, only to have the echidna shred through the seat, burying itself deep in the springs and now you have to get the seats removed to extricate it, further injuring the echidna and costing yourself a lot of money, money you needed to pay for the hay bill to feed the sheep you rescued from slaughter last week, not to mention the vet bills you've undoubtedly acquired.

One aspect in particular that rescuers need to understand is that of quantity over quality. I realised very early on in my horse rescue days that the sheer number of horses needing help were well beyond what any charity or system in the country could contend with. I made a clear decision that my charity would be focused on quality rescue – giving the horse whatever it needed, regardless of the cost, in order for that horse to have the best chance of life in a new home. Adoptions were considered very carefully and occasionally rejected if I didn't feel it was a good long-term fit for that horse. The adoption price was the highest in the country and I refused to lower it for an old or disabled horse, because I never wanted to value one life as worth more than the other.

Other charities do things differently. The RSPCA, for example, works on huge volume (quantity) and there is a need for that too. While I could turn away animals in need, the RSPCA doesn't have that luxury. It fulfils a vital, excruciating role in 'cleaning up' the country's mess of domestic animal overpopulation and the 'throw away' nature of pet ownership. It's not a path I can walk, but someone has to do it. That's how it is at this point in time, though I live in hope that will change in the future.

Maybe you're an experienced rescuer but you can't say no. All of a sudden, your paddocks are overgrazed, you're running out of money for feed, then a drought hits and you have no way of sustaining the cows you rescued. Maybe you took on too many horses, only to have illness or injury strike your family, then comes a sudden drop in income, and you no longer have the ability to financially support them. As well, because you are such a kind-hearted, compassionate person, you took on all the horses no one else wanted, so now you can't even re-home them because, you know, nobody will take them.

I would like to make it very clear here that I've been on all sides of the compassion and wisdom roundabout. Hubby and I are currently calculating the available redraw ability of our home loan and choosing designs to *build a pool* because our newest fur baby has elbow issues and needs ongoing hydrotherapy to improve and maintain quality of life. Yes, *an entire pool* ... because that's how we roll in our house. So, trust me; no judgement here.

The wisdom of limits is something we all must reckon with. I had to truly confront this when I was rescuing horses, slowly adding more to our personal herd, committed to keeping them to the very end of their lives, which we still do. But there was a time when we had six horses and I was fostering a chocolate-brown Shetland pony named Bella, who I had rescued from a meat auction. She was beautifully sweet and gentle and she was best friends with my Shetland gelding, Sparky. I didn't want to separate them and I loved her very much. She was the only foster horse who really broke my heart when I had to say goodbye. But we had to use our wisdom. Taking on another horse was just one horse too many. I didn't want to end up like some of the people who would write to me, begging me to quickly (often in a number of days) find homes for twenty or thirty horses because their marriage had broken down, the property was being sold and their only option was to send the remaining horses to slaughter.

Even today, years after the charity finished its work, I still get phone calls from people asking for help to save a horse. My first instinct every single time is to put up my hand and say, *Yes! I'll take it!* That's my compassion muscle, always wanting to help. But sometimes I wonder, too, if there might not be a bit of ego involved in that reaction. I torture myself (with disturbing emotions) believing that if I don't intervene and take the horse, no one else will and the horse will die. True, that *might* be the result. But it equally might not be. Do I really think I'm the only person in the world who can save that animal? Goodness, what a superhero I must be.

Of course, we never want to be complacent and sit back and think, *Oh, it's okay, someone else will help.* Sometimes, that someone really is you. But sometimes it's not. Here's the Middle Way again, a path we must learn to tread, avoiding the extremes of not ever being able to say no through to never saying yes because you believe another person will step up and do it. That is where we have to practise wisdom.

Discriminating compassion

Living in a rural area of farming industry was both a challenge (if I never again have to drive behind a cattle truck for hours on end, looking at sad faces on their way to slaughter, it will be a welcome relief) but also illuminating. An unexpected awakening for me actually came about when I began to stop seeing the abattoir workers as 'others' and see them instead as people who needed help. Mostly, this wisdom was gained via my husband, who worked as a physio-therapist across a large rural region, frequently attending to people for rehabilitation of workplace injuries acquired in factories and abattoirs.

He would come home and tell me stories of his clients, largely refugee and migrant populations with difficulty speaking English. Some of them were employed illegally (and raids did and do happen in abattoirs across the country for this reason). Many of the injured clients my husband saw had not received the workplace treatment or rehabilitation they deserved by law. Many had no idea how to advocate for themselves (not understanding the Australian medical system, doctors or their rights) or lacked the language ability to do so. One abattoir employed its own (vaguely titled) 'therapist' on site and sent all injured workers through him rather than to external specialists, for reasons I'm sure you can imagine. (If you need explanation, consider that premiums for worker insurance schemes increase with every reported workplace injury.) Some workers were regularly injected with saline as a treatment for serious injuries – and strangely enough no one could explain why salty water was considered an appropriate remedy. Broken bones were missed or mismanaged. A knife-wound through a bicep muscle was bandaged on site so the employee could simply return to work. A man with a broken foot was refused crutches so they put him in a plastic chair, which was wrecking his back.

Hubby once asked me to drop off a moon boot to an injured man so he could continue to work. I drove to the rental house and found no less than four refugee families sharing the one place, the injured man sitting on the concrete under the house, chopping up chicken on a wooden block with a meat cleaver. No one had shoes. No one smiled. Misery dripped from the air. I remember thinking how sad it all was and how desperately unhappy those people looked.

Another time, Hubby was asked to go to a different abattoir. This place had a high rate of injuries and the management team were proactively keen to have Hubby come along to observe practices in the hope he could give advice on minimising the injury rate. When he got there, he was led to the kill floor.

Whoa! He wasn't expecting that.

It was awful, of course, but Hubby has a huge heart for people as well as animals and aside from the pain of watching the animals die, it deeply affected him to see how workers seemed to handle this horrible situation in front of them. He described the employees as falling into two groups – those who seemed blank, silent and shut down, and those who were the total opposite, being loud, joking, jeering and laughing. So many disturbing emotions at play and the Middle Way nowhere in sight.

Aside from the high rates of physical injuries in these places, the emotional trauma must be significant, even if it is pushed out of conscious awareness.

59

Do abattoir workers leave these emotional wounds at work when they go home at the end of a shift? I'm guessing not. That energy must go with them to their families too.

Compassion tells us to advocate for the animals. Wisdom tells us that our compassion shouldn't discriminate and stop at the animals. The people involved in the meat industry may be there for desperate reasons and may not want to be there any more than you or I. They too might dream of a job as a writer, a biologist or designer but have been dealt hands of fate that have blocked those paths for the time being. Sure, some people work there because it's 'just a job' and it doesn't bother them. For others, though, they are there because they have no choice.

If it's true that eating meat is karmically neutral, but that killing an animal is karmically heavy then we as meat eaters are in tremendous spiritual debt to the abattoir workers. They are taking on our karmic debt for us. At the same time that we are advocating for animal rights, wisdom and compassion together may encourage us to advocate for human rights too.

Euthanasia

As we know, suffering exists all the time. It is natural and normal for us to encounter it in our lives and this often means making difficult choices. When it comes to animals, I feel that we are frequently in a position of having to make the best choice out of a handful of bad choices. Buddhism says that to be reborn as an animal is one of the unfortunate rebirths, not because they are any less sentient or worthy, but because they have far fewer choices that are within their control. By extension as their caregivers, this applies to us too. An example of this is to have an animal with a terminal illness. Because the support structures and financial assistance that is in place for humans in such circumstance simply aren't there for animals (Medicare, hospices, home nursing and subsidised medications, for example), the practical ability for what we can do to assist animals through this situation is greatly reduced.

For Buddhists, the issue of euthanasia is a complicated and potentially divisive one. The first precept – do not kill – tells us not to end an animal's life. The wisdom offered to us is that we have no idea what we are doing to an animal's karma when we end their life early and suggests that we are potentially robbing the animal of their chance to work off bad karma through the suffering of their final stages.

I can appreciate that viewpoint and have spent considerable hours and emotions turning it over; however, because I choose to employ wisdom *and* compassion, compassion tells me that we should alleviate suffering wherever we can. Buddhist wisdom says there is no conflict with having a headache and taking a painkiller, so I see no conflict between a suffering and dying animal and the medicine used to alleviate that suffering.

Buddhists say that the way you end your life has the ability to change your experiences in the next life. It's known as completing karma, or finishing karma, which is why so much debate occurs over interventions of euthanasia. I believe that an end of life that is done with love and respect has to be a more peaceful and beneficial way to pass than lying out in the sun while animals attack and kill you slowly while you can do nothing about it . . . just for example.

I will rearrange my life, finances and living situation as much as possible to help an animal through its challenges, but if I've exhausted all my options I will not let an animal suffer. When I brought Daisy home for her last night, she endured hours of seizures that left her whole body contracting rigid, vomiting, with loss of bowel and bladder control, howling. With each seizure she smashed her head into the floor, the wall, the tiles, wherever she happened to be. We couldn't keep her safe. It would have been cruel and negligent to cling to an idea of a 'natural death' in this situation.

I believe that euthanasia – if done lovingly, wisely and compassionately – can be a great gift. Moreover, it might be a chance to teach an animal that it doesn't *have* to suffer. Maybe that very act of courageous kindness (via euthanasia while I kiss and stroke and love her) is the moment that brings her awareness to a higher level. I don't know of course, it's just a feeling.

Make no mistake, I take euthanasia very seriously and I have learned to wait until the moment I get 'the look' from an animal that tells me the time has come. It happens, without fail. The light goes from their eyes and I just *know* – even when I very much don't want to see it, as was the case with my Daisy dog, who caught my eye just as she was sliding down the wall to collapse on the floor.

I think the real test is for us as humans, as loving caregivers, to deal with *our own suffering* at the impending loss of our animal so that we can clearly see what is in front of us and find our mental state calm enough to make the right choices for our animals at the right time.

Spiritual contracts

It is difficult for an animal to earn merit and accrue good karma when their choices come down to situations of having to fight and defend themselves or kill others in order to survive. For this reason, if nothing else, I see it as a tremendous honour and also a significant duty to be mindful at every moment I am with an animal, because my relationship with that animal might be the one and only thing that allows them to experience a reality that propels them towards a higher rebirth.

I believe every animal that comes into my life is here for a reason, and it is my job to work out what that is and support the spiritual contract that has led to our union. Sometimes, we are lucky enough to have an animal with us whose life purpose seems to be

65

blindingly clear. We have one of those living with us now – a cat called Tom. I picked up Tom from the RSPCA, after beginning my day having set the intention that I trusted I'd be taken wherever I needed to be. An hour later, I found myself standing in front of a cage of three ginger-and-white kittens. They were twelve weeks old and according to the description they'd been strays. Two were asleep but the third opened his eyes and stared at me, relentlessly. I took a photo of him and sent it to Hubby, who responded straight away that we had to have him.

At the time, we already had three rescued cats, two dogs and our three-year-old son, and we were all living in a tiny one-hundred-year-old cottage that we'd been renovating, a choice made so we could afford acreage in the area that would allow us to keep the horses. The cottage had transformed from a termite-ridden, falling down house into a rather cute, solid heritage home, which we loved, but which was far too small for us. Intellectual wisdom would say we certainly didn't need yet another animal squashed into that small abode, but our gut (spiritual wisdom) told us we had to take him home.

Our son, Flynn, had been struggling through a tough period, with rising levels of anxiety and fears and an obsessive scratching habit that meant he made his cheek bleed multiple times a day. This had been going on for eight months. I'd taken him to the doctor frequently, despairing over what to do. From the first day Flynn met Tom, he swooped him up into his arms, his face beaming with joy, and carried him around the house. This surprised us because both Hubby and I had been disappointed to find that Tom was decidedly *not* an affectionate cat. When Flynn grabbed hold of Tom, we'd expected the kitten to push him away and struggle until Flynn let go. To our amazement the complete opposite happened and it has been happening every day since.

Flynn drags Tom around the house, lies down with him on his chest and pulls him into his lap to watch television. Occasionally, Tom will evade him but mostly he goes floppy, his eyes glaze over and he purrs and purrs. (The other day, I walked into the lounge room to find Flynn and Tom snuggled up against one another, eyes closed, having a rest inside the dog crate.) I have scores of photos of Flynn and Tom together, precisely because every day that we see this relationship in action we stop whatever we're doing to watch. It's like magic.

Within six weeks of bringing Tom into our house, Flynn had completely stopped scratching at his face. Tom still doesn't like anyone else to pat or hold him, but he has an entirely different set of rules just for Flynn. Every week we thank Tom for being such an unexpected and amazing friend for Flynn and it is obvious to us that Tom is earning considerable merit in this lifetime by helping our son.

This is an example of when the wisdom–compassion struggle can be so tricky. 'Rational' wisdom would have told us that we were mad to bring another animal into our small home. Sometimes, though, spiritual wisdom goes beyond logical thought. Time and again we see that rarely is anything black and white.

When doing right feels bad

Our experience with Tom is a beautiful thing. Sadly, there are many more times when doing the right thing is far from simple or straightforward. Rats and mice pose a particular struggle for me and it's a situation where compassion and wisdom have to wrestle it out.

In 2007 when I saw His Holiness the Dalai Lama, he spoke at length about compassion for animals. Then he started giggling and said something like, 'But you know that sound, at night, when you're lying in bed, trying to sleep, and you're just drifting off and then hear *zzzzzzzzz*?' He made the high-pitched

69

sound of a mosquito. Then he laughed heartily. 'Ah, compassion for mosquito, veee-ry difficult.' He sat there in his robes, chuckling away and I laughed with him, buoyed that even the Dalai Lama struggles with these everyday issues.

Two years after that, we had a mouse plague invade our house. I was determined not to kill them. I tried bargaining with them – I was happy for them to live outside in the hay shed – but they didn't see reason. They kept multiplying. I bought electronic soundwave devices to plug into the wall, which were supposed to shoo them away. They had no effect whatsoever. I bought catch-and-release traps and set them up and began to catch cute, small brown creatures that I then let go over the fence and into the neighbours' paddock. (Don't worry, there was one hundred acres between the fence and his house.) But still they multi-plied faster than I could catch and release.

They were in the linen cupboard and I had to wash everything. They were all through the kitchen cupboards and I had to pull everything out and wash them and disinfect the shelves to get rid of the poop and urine. Then I had to do it again. And again. By the third time, I was ready to kill them.

Then I heard the Dalai Lama's voice. 'Compassion for mosquito, veee-ry difficult.' I saw his face laughing, and I laughed too.

Fortunately, my third round of catch-and-release and full kitchen cleaning, as well as plugging some gaps around pipes into the house, worked. I had won that battle.

Ten years later, when it was obvious that there were rats in our ceiling, I went through similar efforts. I tried talking to them first (they are known for being quite smart, after all) and I explained that I didn't want to kill them but they had to leave the house. Then I went with the plug-in device into the wall. Then I considered catch-and-release traps, but they were so big and I'd have had to climb up into the ceiling every day to check them (and I knew I couldn't do that).

As well, I'm fairly frightened of rats and I couldn't imagine being able to handle them. I went into denial and I ignored every sound of gnawing and scampering and scratching I heard, hoping beyond hope that I would wake up one day and they'd be gone.

But they didn't go away.

I was in agony until wisdom kicked in. I knew the dangers of having rats in the house, not least of which was their destruction of wiring and the potential for danger. What if a fire started one day while we were out and we had cats and dogs locked inside? Would I be content to know that I'd saved the rats' lives only to kill our own animals? Or what if the fire started at night and killed our son, or us? Was that okay? Clearly, it wasn't.

I killed the rats. Was I happy about it? Absolutely not. Did I feel terrible? Yes. But was it the right thing to do? Yes, I believe so. Suffering exists. There is rarely a perfect solution. Sometimes, wisdom says, the only thing you can do is minimise the suffering and make the best choice out of two bad options. Sorry, dear rats.

Another example of this kind happened to us when I spontaneously rescued chicks from my son's kindergarten, which had just finished with an egg-hatching program. The woman from the business that supplied the chicks came to the classroom, where the eggs had sat under warming lights until they hatched, and the kids had watched them get up and about on their feet for a couple of weeks. Now it was time for the chicks to go. She scooped them up and put them in a cardboard box, which she happened to place at my feet as I was sitting outside. I heard the cheeping.

'What's in there?'

'Two-week old chicks. You want them? We've got no use for them. We're giving them away.'

Oh, how my rescuing heart bled for those chicks. They were excess, sentient collateral, and half of them would be roosters, which no one wanted. I could only imagine what was to become of those unwanted chicks. I said I'd take four.

I knew there was a good chance that at least two of them would turn out to be roosters, but Hubby and I agreed we would simply build another pen for the roosters to live in. Just down the road from us, the local garbage tip has become a literal dumping ground for unwanted roosters and the verge of the road is peppered with all manner of fowl ambling around. Every now and then, the council comes around and 'cleans them up', taking them away for disposal. We'd talked about starting a rooster rescue, only to conclude (via wisdom) that it wouldn't work because nobody would be willing to adopt them. With no desexing options out there for roosters, they simply became pests.

Never mind, we reasoned, we would look after our roosters we took home that day and they could live out their life with us. We invested several hundred dollars in building them their own yard and rooster house – a considerable investment for 'free chicks' – because that's the kind of crazy people we are.

Sadly, it turned out to be what we considered our first ever rescue fail. Two chicks grew up into handsome roosters and we dutifully separated them into their own pen. But we couldn't keep them in. At first they flew over the fence, so we clipped their wings. Then they simply climbed the fence. Once out, they stalked us. They attacked our son, visitors and our dogs. We were all terrified to walk out the door. When they weren't attacking us, they were attacking each other, inflicting terrible wounds, or if they managed to climb their own fence and then the hens' fence, they attacked and harassed the girls. During the times they were inside their own pen, and not actively fighting or assaulting each other, they were utterly miserable, pacing up and down the fence line until they'd dug themselves a trench two inches deep.

Finally, we had to accept that they couldn't stay. There was nowhere else for them to go – unless people were going to breed from them (furthering the cycle of unwanted chicks) or eat them. We made the rather heartbreaking decision to euthanise them down at our local vet practice. Releasing them at the local dump might seem like a nice idea to others, but the outcome for an abandoned rooster was a life fighting other roosters, being attacked by snakes, foxes and wild dogs, being hit by a car on the road, or eventually being rounded up by the council and disposed of in whatever way they saw fit. We knew the fate that lay in store for our roosters. We did love them. Euthanasia was the best of a bunch of bad options. Was it better for them to have come to us even for a short time to know a little bit of love and life before death, or to have been deemed as 'waste products' as chicks and put to death then? I might never know.

So . . . back to meat eating

The purpose of all these examples is to show that our complicated relationship with animals doesn't start and end with whether or not we eat them. It's easy to get fixated on this one action, but there is a whole spectrum of opportunities to employ wisdom and compassion each and every day, just as the meanest vegan I ever met showed me. Was it okay for him to abstain from animal products but then torment my animals and rant and bully the people around him? I don't think so.

With many reports claiming cigarette butts are a bigger source of ocean pollution than plastic straws or bags, is it still better to be vegan but continue to smoke cigarettes, more than five trillion of which are produced each year?

Is it okay for you to beat yourself up for not being good enough when you eat meat, when you might actually be dedicating your life to animals in all sorts of other ways?

It's important that we don't latch onto guilt (attachment) as a substitute for compassion, or throw in the towel and give up on compassionate acts because we feel we failed in one area. Compassion tells me I'd rather choose to not eat meat. Wisdom says (in an increasingly louder voice until I listen) that I tried for decades and my health suffered every time. I might save four thousand animals in my lifetime by being vegan (while remembering that all food production kills thousands of animals on top of that, even vegetarian diets), while being fatigued and sick, whereas by eating the meat I need and being healthy, vibrant and productive, I might start a worldwide animal charity, raise hundreds of thousands of dollars for animal causes, launch education or political campaigns that change the future of farming, write books that are read by many thousands of people who also go out and spread compassionate action and change the lives of hundreds of thousands of animals. If I purchased a tract of land and revegetated it with koala food trees and it became the very last area on which koalas could live and breed, thereby saving the entire species from extinction, would that make up for eating meat?

I could also go online and argue with people, firebomb buildings, or sit in a corner and drill down the statistics of how much blood was on my hands and give myself a stomach ulcer, spiralling into a deep depression from which I never recovered and was never functional again. Would that make up for eating meat?

This is deliberately provocative and I hope you realise this: I have no clue how it all works . . . and neither do you. That's the point. We're *all* just trying to do our best and make a difference in the way that we are called to make a difference, and no one can tell you what that 'weighs' on the spiritual scales. No one can tell you if you are doing a good enough job because no one knows.

Give yourself a break. Give the vegan a break. Give the meat eater a break. Give the farmer a break. Give the abattoir worker a break. Give the activist a break. Give your cat a break. Give the cranky horse a break. Give your spouse a break. Be generous with the breaks.

You never know when you'll need one too and you'll never know when that very act of kindness could change the world.

Journal Questions

1. Have you ever had an experience of compassion without wisdom? How did it impact your life and the lives of those around you?

2. Have you ever wished you *had* acted in a certain situation, rather than waiting for someone else to step in?

3. Have you ever overcommitted to a cause? What was the end result?

4. Think of situations where you hold ideas of 'otherness' about people. If you bring those to mind now, how does it make you feel? Is there some way to close the gap between you and 'the other'?

Practical Challenge

o Close the gap just a little between you and an 'other'. You might be able to start a conversation with someone who seems to be a world removed from your life experience. If not, perhaps you could try imagining yourself in that person's shoes, seeing things from their perspective. Perhaps you could even simply research online in order to read someone's personal story about a situation, to read their own words as they describe what their life is like and why they feel the way they do.

o If you are currently overcommitted, find one thing you can do to relieve some pressure off yourself in that situation. If you can't change anything immediately, decide on a new boundary (using your wisdom) for the future.

Five

Mindfulness
for Meat Eaters:
Here's how you can win!

Do you rush around? Do you find yourself thinking that the day has just flown by and you've no idea what you've done? Do you ever say things you wish you hadn't or get into conflict with someone over nothing? Chances are you weren't being mindful. Don't worry, you're not alone. We only have to spend a couple of seconds contemplating all the awful things going on in the world to realise that most of us are not acting mindfully.

Last year, I discovered that 'rushing' was pretty much the cause of every issue in my life. Rushing around to get things done leads to injury. Rushing through conversations while multitasking leads to miscommunications. Rushing while driving leads to accidents, road rage and speeding tickets. Rushing while consuming food leads to overeating, poor choices and indigestion. On and on it goes.

Meditation is the core practice of Buddhism and mindfulness is the foundation of a meditation practice. The definition of mindfulness is being totally and wholly aware of the present moment. The simplest way to do this is to close your eyes and breathe, focusing on the in-breath, following it all the way to the end, then focusing on the out-breath, following it all the way to the end, and repeating. Like almost everything in Buddhism, it sounds so simple and yet is so shockingly complex. I can barely make it to three full breaths before my mind has jumped elsewhere.

Most of us would have heard someone (perhaps a yoga instructor, or a psychologist, or a guru of some kind) say, 'Clear your mind,' or 'Let all the thoughts drift away.' We try to do it – and fail in two seconds flat. Then what happens? We get frustrated. We berate ourselves. And then we give up.

Although I have meditated in one form or another for decades, I have only recently come to truly understand the real goal in meditating.

The goal is *not* to empty your mind.

We've all been doing it wrong

In *First, We Make the Beast Beautiful*, author Sarah Wilson describes a moment she got to interview His Holiness the Dalai Lama and ask him one question. She asked him how she could get her mind to shut up. His response?

85

'There's no use . . . Silly! Impossible to achieve!'

Yes, that was from *the Dalai Lama*! This is where we've been getting it wrong. The goal of meditation is not to shut off thoughts, but to actually notice, observe and witness them instead. With the exception of a few masters of mindfulness, such as Eckhart Tolle (*The Power of Now*), who might be able to halt their stream of incessant thoughts, the rest of us need to work on it, every minute of every day – and by work, I mean try, fail, and try again.

The goal is to build up our mental muscle to notice the distracting thought, the distracting sound, the distracting itch or the distracting heat or cold, to let it pass like clouds drifting across the sky, and then come back to the present. You might be relieved to realise that the more thoughts you have, the more opportunity you have to build mental muscle.

Used in Buddhism is the metaphor that our mind is the sky, but the thoughts are the clouds. Sometimes, our minds are beautiful, clear blue skies, and sometimes dark and stormy. But the sky itself never changes – just the clouds. In observing the clouds, we see the changing nature of our thoughts and take comfort that storms come and go but the sky endures, untouched.

At times during meditation, the goal is to notice those distracting thoughts (clouds) and sit with them until they change, thereby teaching our-selves in the most powerful way that all things change – impermanence.

I'm terribly itchy. I have dry skin that itches and itches, and I often joke that I'm like an old dog that will take all the scratching you can give it and groan with relief while you do it, its back leg waving in the air in response. My husband knows I'm always itchy so when he greets me, he automatically scratches my back. (That's love, I tell you.) When I meditate, I itch even more because I am aware of it. This used to be a real point of frustration for me, until I learned to actually observe the itch on my back. Then I would move my attention down to my leg. Was it itching there too? Yes, it was. But you know what? In moving my attention to my leg, I no longer felt the itching on my back. Then I moved attention to my feet, scalp, arms. What sensations were there? Tingling, heat, pulsating. But I no longer itched on my back or leg.

This was such an illuminating experience for me. Soon after I started practising this type of mindfulness, I had to have an MRI. Anyone who's had an MRI will know that you have to lie perfectly still for a long stretch of time. Sometimes, they want you to take shallow breaths and sometimes, as in the one I did for my sinuses, they even want you to avoid swallowing properly. I can tell you that the moment someone says, 'Try not to swallow,' you will produce litres of saliva that trickle to the back of your throat and demand to be swallowed.

So there I was, having to be completely still, having to breathe shallow breaths and not swallow, while of course I felt like I'd drown in saliva, every part of me was itching, my right arm was going numb, all while I was strapped into head pieces and zoomed into a narrow, claustrophobic tube while deafening bangs and knocks and jackhammer sounds hurt my ears despite the headphones.

The only thing I could do was meditate. I focused on my breathing. I felt into every itch, pain, throb or feeling that was going on and when I thought I couldn't stand not to shift or wiggle I moved my attention to another spot to observe the feeling there, while the previous feeling subsided. Everything changed. Panic subsided. Calm ensued, so much so that I was quite seriously nearly asleep by the time they whizzed me out of that tube. I was so grateful I'd built up my meditation muscles to help in that moment.

My next appointment at the dentist went in a similar manner. I hate going to the dentist, as I'm sure many people do. I get so nervous and so stressed and this time I had to have a very small but rather painful hole filled in a tooth. My heart raced for days beforehand, imagining the pain. I wasn't even experiencing the pain and yet my mind had already done the job of creating the anxiety and difficulty for me. The day before the appointment, I made a decision. Instead of dreading and fearing the dentist, I would focus on gratitude that I live in a country where I can get quality dental care at all and have it done quickly before that tiny hole turned into a huge one, maybe an abscess, a root canal or tooth extraction. Every time I noticed fear, I turned my attention to gratitude and to the many people around the world who can't afford dental care or get access to it, and felt compassion for their pain and suffering instead of my own anxiety.

It helped. I was still nervous, but I was aware of my thoughts and could choose how I handled them. In the end, the *anticipation* of the pain had been far worse than the actual pain of the injections, which lasted mere minutes, rather than the days of mental torture I'd endured while I imagined all sorts of things that never eventuated.

These are a couple of examples of the way in which mindfulness can help us get through parts of our lives. Of course, mindfulness is a muscle – the more we use it, the stronger it gets. Ten minutes of meditation a day (even five, if that's what you can manage) is far more effective than trying to do hours at a time once a week. Little and often is all we need to start training our minds to do what we want them to, rather than our minds leading us down crazy, dark tunnels. The key, of course, is to start this mind training before you are in a crisis. Learning to deal with an uncomfortable MRI is one thing; learning to deal with a serious health diagnosis or the loss of a loved one is something else. These are the moments in which hundreds of accumulated hours of meditation can help, allowing you to practise mindfulness when you most need it.

Meditation in motion

One of my favourite teachers is Thich Nhat Hanh, a hugely loved Zen Buddhist monk, originally from Vietnam, who was exiled for speaking out against the war in his home country. Within the many schools of Buddhism, Zen Buddhism is the one I relate to the most. The nature of Zen is to strip away and simplify, and Thich Nhat Hanh does this beautifully by placing the focus of his practice and teachings on the present moment, wherever you are and whatever you're doing. I've read that to be a Zen Buddhist, you only really need to believe in three things: the Buddha, the cycle of rebirth, and karma. That sits well with me.

Thich Nhat Hanh has written dozens of books and he is passionate about mindfulness in everyday moments. We tend to think of mindfulness and meditation as a quiet, still activity, and this is certainly valid. But Thich Nhat Hanh is a firm believer in moving meditation. He has said that it can take him a full hour to drink a cup of tea. He practises walking meditations, repeating phrases in his mind with every step he takes. He respects the art of washing the dishes as a wonderful opportunity to practise mindfulness, and he strongly urges us to eat our food mindfully, something I'm guessing very few of us do well.

For me, eating mindfully is a challenge, one that I will frequently notice I'm not doing, and then quickly dismiss it as being too difficult or taking too much time. (It's crazy how we can sabotage ourselves so easily.) I know this is, without doubt, an important aspect of my life that I need to work on.

I often eat and drink while I'm working at my desk, or driving in the car, or while I'm simultaneously having conversations with other people, or making my son's lunch to take to school, or getting dressed, or watching television, or scrolling on my phone. Eating is an activity that we can, functionally speaking, do while we do other things. We tend to rush food or think of it as an inconvenience (getting something 'quick' or 'on the go'). These days, with so much food readily available to pluck off the shelf in the supermarket, we don't even have a true connection to where the food came from in the first place. We don't have to work for it (literally, with our hands in the dirt) and so our appreciation for it is naturally lower than it would be had we waited two years for that pineapple. (*Two years* for a pineapple? That I can then pick up for two dollars! Anyone else thinking we need to pay our farmers more?) With meat, if we're not killing the animal ourselves, it is all too easy to look at some mince or stir-fry strips and have no real appreciation for where it came from.

Now, I'm not suggesting that you flagellate yourself and make yourself sick and weepy with guilt before you eat the meat. None of that is useful. But how often do you thank the animal that gave its life for you to have that food? Once a year? Every day? Monthly? Three times in your life? Or with every single meal? Few of us, I'm certain, would do it each meal time.

Remember, it's not just that particular animal that has given its life for us to have that food. The vegetables gave their lives too, as did all the small insects that died in the farming process. And then there are the farmers, the abattoir workers, the transporters, and the seller, not to mention the person who cooked it for you. Truly, how often do you genuinely thank the person who cooks your food, truly showing gratitude, not just with a reflex 'thanks'? So many lives and hands have touched the food that ends up on your plate, which then goes into your body to nourish you, sustain you, heal you and transform your cells every day.

When I was quite sick with fatigue in 2005, I used to head into the city to attend the Hare Krishna restaurant's Sunday afternoon dinners. I loved it there. They told us that the three pillars of their faith were feasting, dancing and chanting. (Seriously, what's not to love about that?) They are vegetarian and they would serve up a wonderful meal after the chanting and dancing. I was most impressed to learn that great importance was given to ensuring the food was prepared with peace, calm and love, recognising that this energy was transmitted to the people who ate it. I really savoured my time there, and that particular piece of wisdom resounded deeply in me.

Many traditions around the world have their own version of offering thanks, or 'grace'. You might like to adopt one (an internet search will bring up many different varieties) or come up with one of your own. They range from the very simple ('Thanks' or 'Grace') to the very complex (long passages of prayers and remembrance).

When I remember to do it (I'm still practising because I know how important it is), I usually go with something like:

I give thanks to the animals and plants that have given their lives so that I may have this food.

But thinking about it more deeply, I recognise that I'd like to acknowledge our farmers and growers too, who often choose a life that is not easy and often not even particularly profitable, all because they believe in what they do. So, I now adjust mine to say:

I give thanks to the growers and carers of this food, and to the animals and plants that have given their lives so that I may benefit from this meal.

Just saying this, either mentally or out loud, brings about a 'drop' in me. I feel my energies move from the whirlwind of my mind to the steady calm of my heart. I truly feel a part of the huge web of life that has brought this nourishment to my plate.

In our family, we also use meal times together to talk about our three favourite moments of the day, thereby linking food, family and gratitude together. Gratitude goes a long way towards mindfulness. If you keep a gratitude journal, you might like to start including your love for the foods you eat. I keep gratitude journals sporadically, writing in them every night for months, then falling off that wagon for months, then starting again. But when I write about food, I definitely feel a deeper connection to food that is about more than just how delicious it was. Each piece of fruit or vegetable is nothing short of a miracle.

There are specific Buddhist prayers and blessings for food and even for eating meat. If you do an online search, you will find them. I won't copy them here because I don't want to offend any one particular school of Buddhist thought, and as I don't use them myself I don't feel it would be a wise thing to do, but they are out there. If you are in touch with Buddhist monks and nuns, you could also ask them to help you with specific prayers and blessings on this.

Mindful purchasing

The act of buying food is a fantastic opportunity to practise mindfulness. You can learn to *feel* food and most people will be able to notice the difference between the feel of food that is in a supermarket, and which has probably been in storage for months, or come from overseas (and possibly chemically treated before it was released into the country) and fresh produce from farmers markets. It's tangible.

Where you buy your food and how much thought you put into it is so important. If you want to help save the earth and animals, then choosing organic produce is obviously your best choice, given how much synthetic chemicals do to the environment and its inhabitants. Buying locally produced food is also a no-brainer, as it means lower carbon footprints through lower food miles and it also means your food is as fresh as you can find it without growing it yourself. Of course, growing as much of your own food as you can is wonderful too and it means you can utilise that nutritious compost we're all supposed to be making in order to reduce greenhouse gas emissions.

Meat that has been raised free range goes some way to improving the life of the animal, though it can be a tricky thing to monitor. For instance, free range eggs are notorious for not accurately describing what a chicken's life is really like, because there is currently no legal definition of what 'free range' means in terms of number of birds per hectare or their access to pastures and sunshine, for example. Organically raised meat is, by definition, free range (though, again, the actual conditions of what that means does vary).

A garbage truck of rubbish enters the ocean every minute of the day

This would also be a good time to talk about plastics. Yes, most Australian states have finally come in line with many countries around the world and banned single-use plastic bags at the checkout. But I'm sure I'm not the only one who still sees an alarming amount of plastic walking out the door at the shops. A single zucchini wrapped up on a styrofoam tray and covered in cling film is a truly disturbing sight.

I get my fruit and vegetables delivered via an amazing business called Fresh Box, which sources the best (I have seriously never seen food so fresh in my life) local produce. If I do buy from the organic superstore, my food comes home in recycled cardboard boxes. Boxes are always a great alternative if you can get them (my local IGA now gives them away instead of bags) and these make fabulous 'blankets' to smother weeds in the garden, which means you don't have to use awful weedkillers that harm our precious bees. Just lay them down over the weeds, then cover them with mulch or straw and no one will even see them. They'll last a long time too, breaking down slowly and keeping your garden neat in the meantime. If you don't have a garden, boxes are easily recyclable.

The amount of packaging around food disturbs me. Seaweed snacks, especially. There is an insane amount of waste around those paper-thin seaweed papers! Food aimed at kids is often the worst. My son's school has started a 'waste free' day once a week, encouraging parents to pack lunchboxes with package-free foods. A fabulous array of lunchboxes and bento boxes are out there now, leaving little excuse to be wrapping up food in plastic anymore.

Buying food in bulk from wholefood superstores also saves in packaging. You can mostly scoop and pour into paper bags and then store in glass jars in your home. My friend Ashley is a huge advocate of big glass jars because you can see exactly what healthy food you have at your fingertips at any given time. When it's in sight it's in mind, which to my way of thinking is mindfulness made easy.

Alternatives to plastic wrap are popping up all over the place, including beeswax wraps, paper bags and containers with lids. I love my cloth vegetable bags (brand name, The Swag), which come in various sizes and do a good job of keeping vegetables fresh. You simply wet them with water and place your produce inside, leaving food lasting for longer. I used to think vegetables wilted because they got old, but it's actually because they lose water. When the bags get dirty, I just throw them in the washing machine and they're ready to go again. These are so simple and effective, and make me feel way better about my health and the environment from avoiding all that plastic being in contact with my food.

Plastics and The Big Five

When it comes to plastics, the first five to deal with are:

- cigarette butts
- plastic bags
- straws
- water bottles
- takeaway coffee cups.

If you do nothing but entirely eliminate these five items from the rest of your life, you'd be doing a wonderful thing.

> If you have accepted that you are 'failing' in the not-eating-meat goals of your life, then *this* right here is the place where you can win!

In 2015 it was widely reported that ninety per cent of seabirds were found to have plastic in their stomachs. Every piece of plastic made since the 1950s still exists and will outlive us and our kids and probably our grandchildren. Spend a couple of minutes googling 'plastic in the ocean' and you'll be horrified at the rate at which we're smothering ourselves in this. Recycling cannot stop it. Cleaning it up might mitigate certain targeted areas, but we will never get it all out. We have to stop it at the source.

As I am writing this, a deceased whale has washed up in Indonesia with more than six kilograms of plastic in its stomach, including more than one hundred drinking cups, twenty-five plastic bags, as well as flip-flops, plastic bottles and hundreds of other bits of plastic. It is devastating evidence of the appalling way we have abused our earth and its living inhabitants.

So much of our reckless use of plastics comes down to a matter of mindfulness (or rather, mindlessness) and a willingness to put the planet first before our own temporary convenience – and I say temporary, because once our planet is polluted beyond repair that's not going to be particularly convenient for any of us.

Australia throws away around a billion coffee cups each year. Staggering, isn't it? If you're the kind of person who can carry reusable coffee cups around with you, this is a great alternative to takeaway cups (because even the supposedly recyclable cups have plastic linings that don't break down). I can imagine this option would suit people who work in offices, for example, where you can just keep your cup on your desk, go outside and get your fill, then take it back to the office to wash and replace on your desk in time for the next cuppa.

I've tried this system, but it doesn't work for me. Personally, I've found that the best thing is to do what they did in the old days and *stay still* for five or ten minutes to drink the coffee in house. I know, it's almost unthinkable these days. But staying still to drink the coffee does several things: it means you don't have to carry your cup around and inevitably forget it and then get cranky; there's no chance of a dripping cup and having it leak in your car or bag; you don't have to then remember to get it out of the car or your bag to wash it and dry it and have it back in your car or bag for the next time; and possibly, most importantly, it gives you a fabulous opportunity to *drink mindfully* rather than gulping on the run or while you're driving. If you wanted to be extra crazy, you could even avoid scrolling on your phone for the minutes it takes you to drink your coffee, focus on your breathing, focus on tasting your coffee, listing the things you're grateful for, observing humankind, or talking with someone, giving them your undivided attention and mindfully listening.

Now, plastic water bottles. Alas, I confess that while I've been good on the other big five plastic items, water bottles have taken me longer to sort out.

I've given up straws and have the metal ones with the little tiny brushes to clean inside them (which is tedious, but I take inspiration from Thich Nhat Hanh that anything tedious is really just a great opportunity for mindfulness), but it's taken me a while to fix my long-held habits with water.

My problem was that although I carried water around with me, I would run out, or I would forget it and then I'd get thirsty, so I would buy water. My other issue was that I'm quite sensitive to water and can smell the chemicals in it long before it's reached my lips, and it makes me feel sick. I usually get 'traveller's belly' wherever I go and it's not normally from food but from the water – even if it's just Sydney or Melbourne. I've finally sorted this out by buying a water bottle with an inbuilt filtering system, and while that bottle is made of BPA-free plastic (I haven't yet found a stainless steel one), I will have it for many years and save hundreds of throwaway plastic bottles.

The other thing to do, if you get caught out some-where and have to buy a drink, is to only buy glass bottles or aluminium cans as these can be recycled forever, unlike plastic.

If you're a smoker, cigarette butts contain plastics in the filters and never break down. In 2018, it was again widely reported that new studies found that cigarette butts were actually the *biggest* source of pollutants in the ocean. I'm not a smoker, so I don't claim to know how difficult or otherwise it might be to give up the habit, so if you're a smoker, I'm just going to leave this here for you to mindfully work out how you can best help the earth when it comes to your butts.

Whether it's plastic bags, coffee cups or cigarette butts, it's clear that they are all very, very bad.

If your focus is more on animals than on the environment, you might be wondering what this has to do with helping the world's creatures. The answer is that everything is connected. All that plastic ends up in our oceans and kills our turtles, dugongs, dolphins, birdlife, fish, octopuses and whales, among others. If you can't give up meat, you can certainly give up plastic. Because I quit my degree that involved a lot of statistics, I cannot possibly do the maths on this, but I think it would be comparatively *interesting* to know how many animal lives you could spare each year by giving up plastic versus giving up meat. Again, if you can't save the animals from meat production you can absolutely save them from dying slow and painful deaths via plastic.

Lastly, committing to improving our actions around plastics requires us to be mindful, and mindfulness is the building block of a compassionate and wise life.

Practical challenges

Here are some ways to apply mindfulness when it comes to food.

- Create your own blessing or ritual that feels good for you to use when you approach each meal.

- Eat your food in silence, alone, sitting outside in nature.

- Put your fork or spoon down between each mouthful.

- Chew your mouthful twenty times (counting is great mindfulness) before swallowing.

- Use the time it takes to boil the kettle for some mindful minutes, concentrating on your breathing, noticing thoughts and letting them go, observing sensations in your body.

- Keep a food diary, noting what you eat and drink each day and any body sensations that surface, such as indigestion, tightness, bloating, cramps, headaches, eczema, irritability and insomnia.

(Conversely, what made you feel great?) Do it for two weeks, then see if you can connect any foods with any symptoms.

- Turn off the television. Turn off your phones (and don't bring them to the table). Light some candles. Play soft music. 'Set' the table as you might for guests. Treat this meal as special, because it is.

- Drink your coffee on your own, without distractions, just observing life.

- Do a 'health check' on your buying habits. How many plastics did you bring home? Are there alternatives on hand? Do you know where your local organic and wholefood stores are?

- Go through each room in your home and find alternatives to every last piece of plastic. Start replacing them one by one. For example, you'll find many plastic items in your bathroom. These days, you can replace shampoo and conditioner bottles with bars (like soap bars) to wash your

111

hair; you can replace your toothbrushes with ones made from bamboo, your liquid soap with bars and your cotton buds with bamboo alternatives. In the kitchen, you can replace synthetic sponges with bamboo scourers and cut up old towels and t-shirts to use as cleaning cloths. You can buy your dishwasher tablets from a brand that uses cardboard packaging instead of plastic. You can now buy child-friendly (or pool-friendly) cups and plates made of bamboo instead of plastic. Once you start looking, you'll find many items you can replace with environmentally respons- ible alternatives. Commit to that journey.

o Invest in good quality glass jars for your pantry. (Having perfect seals is the key to making this work, as this will make food last longer. Fido jars, which use a rubber gasket and a metal clamp to ensure an airtight seal, are fabulous.) Buy in bulk and fill them up.

- Purchase from your nearest organic butcher or at least a specialty butcher with grass-fed, local produce.

Six

Judgement:
Round and round we go

If you're a meat eater who feels guilty, you might be sensitive to judgement from the vegan and vegetarian communities because you already feel a sense of shame, which is triggered by what others think of you. If you were an arrogantly happy carnivore, you wouldn't care less. The fact that you feel a strong response to Facebook posts of animals in horrible conditions or statistics on how many animals you eat a year or how easily you could save the planet if you just stopped eating meat, shows you that you care. Still, it never feels good.

There are different types of judgement. One of these is our ability to assess a situation for risks or benefits. We use our 'good judgement' to make 'good decisions'. But we are also familiar with the other type of judgement – random, wounding criticism from others. That type of judgement is destructive and often comes with the intent to harm, the intent to force an opinion on you and change you, the intent to prove that the hurler of this judgement is 'right'. You only have to spend a few minutes on social media to see this playing out in every hour of the day.

Destructive judgement hurts, in all sorts of ways. Our reaction to it is generally swift and the powerful emotions of anger, fear, fury, frustration and revenge may fly to the surface faster than we can blink. Our first response is often to defend ourselves, try to prove that judgement wrong, or simply to hurl the abuse back to the source. Alternatively, it might be a slow building of these emotions, developed over time in a toxic relationship.

I once watched a video online about a man who had rescued a calf from slaughter and delivered him to an animal shelter. I remember the woman on the video (who worked at the shelter) expressing how shocked she was that a meat eater had saved the calf and taken the time to get him to them. I felt so outraged on the man's behalf, and by extension my own, because I ate meat but I regularly rescued animals. Just because I (or he) eats meat, doesn't mean we're monsters! We still have the ability to feel compassion and a desire to help others. The shelter woman's incredulous amazement that a meat eater could show such kindness for an animal was offensive. Moreover, isn't that what animal lovers want? People who care and rescue? I'm still baffled by this reaction today (and clearly have a wee bit more processing to do about that one).

As a meat eater, I am sensitive to others' judgements about meat eating. But as a writer, I am sensitive to others' judgements about the quality of my work. As a woman, I am sensitive to others' judgements about how I look, act or speak, or the way they describe me, and on it goes. Any area of our life is open to judgement from others. No matter what you are doing, someone will always be there to judge you.

But how do we deal with it in a constructive way?

His Holiness the Dalai Lama still feels anger but, unlike most of us, he knows what to do with it, so he wrote a book entitled *Healing Anger: The Power of Patience from a Buddhist Perspective*. In many interviews, he has stressed that the worst thing you can do with anger is to try to supress it. That doesn't mean that you act out your furious, revengeful fantasies and engage in keyboard wars online. It means you find practical ways to diffuse it.

The very first step is to take time. How often have you said something in the heat of the moment only to regret it later? Physically remove yourself from a tense situation if you need to. I heard a story of a time when Thich Nhat Hanh was speaking in America, encouraging an end to the war in Vietnam. A man in the audience heckled him, demanding to know why he was here and talking rather than back in Vietnam helping his people. Nhat Hanh went silent for a while, apparently dealing with his immediate emotional response to this question, then gave a beautifully elegant response, before quickly leaving the stage to recompose himself. This is such a powerful example of how important it is to take time to process our emotions instead of instantly responding to anger with anger. Even Zen masters still need to do it.

When I was a wannabe vegan, I tried to join a vegetarian society, hoping that by hanging out with vegetarians I would learn more about how to make the transition. But I was denied. In order to join, I had to sign a document stating that I'd abstained from animal foods for six weeks before I would be admitted. The door had been slammed in my face. I remember feeling hurt – *I wasn't good enough* – and angry – *how did they expect to encourage vegetarianism if they wouldn't welcome people who were trying?* Exclusion is a form of judgement and all it did was make me want to tell them where to go, and I probably had a good rant about it to a few people too.

At one point, I was seeing a counsellor to help me through a time of life transition and she said to me, 'Do you realise that no matter how hard you work, and no matter how good your work is, that someone will always find fault in it?'

I was shocked into silence.

No, I had never even considered that. I'd sincerely believed that if I worked hard enough, if I kept improving and giving my best and doing everything 'right', then everything would be just fine. Was it really true that someone would always find something they thought was 'wrong'? This was a big moment for me and broke down my long-held belief in how the world worked. I had to accept that judgement would keep coming my way no matter what, and I had to find a way to make peace with it.

Dealing with judgement

Here are some tips to help you navigate your way through judgement from others.

1. **Accept that judgement happens.** (Remember the First Noble Truth? Suffering exists.) In this sense, we shouldn't be shocked when we are confronted by judgement. In fact, we should be more inclined to say, 'Oh, judgement, here you are, right on time!'

2. **Recognise your immediate response.** There is no point trying to deny it. Name it. 'Oh, anger/grief/ humiliation/devastation/mortification, here you are, right on time!'

3. **Take your time.** Most of us instinctively respond to defend ourselves. This is natural, right?

Judgements and criticisms are attacks. If we were being physically attacked by a wild animal, we'd want to defend ourselves. Judgements are psychological attacks, so we will want to act out. But meeting anger with anger is the worst possible response. Anger begets anger, on and on and on. Remove yourself from the situation if you can – leave the room, leave work early, go for a drive, turn off your phone and the computer. Give yourself *at least* twenty-four hours before responding (if you need to at all).

4. **Deal with the emotions.** Exercise is a fabulous way to deal with emotions. When we feel an emotional response to a psychological attack, our body produces cortisol (stress hormone) and adrenaline (fight or flight). These hormones need somewhere to go. Use them. Go and dig in the garden. Go for a long walk. Swim laps. Jog. Do some vigorous housework. Crazy dance in your kitchen. My personal favourite is to shovel out the stable.

I think the symbolism of getting rid of the manure in my life is quite cathartic.

5. **Mental investigation.** Once you've helped your physical body process its hormones, turn to your mental state. Consider the judgement that has been offered. Can you see anything in it that has even a tiny spark of truth? Can you identify what it is about the judgement that has triggered you? What are you attached to? (Remember, attachments are the cause of all suffering.) Are you attached to the need for external validation? Are you attached to a fantasy you had about how you might have been received? Is it your pride that has been wounded? Are you attached to ideas about how other people should behave? (And might that therefore be a reflection of your own judgement?)

Don't be afraid to seek professional guidance. There is absolutely no conflict between Buddhism and medical or psychological assistance from professionals. Indeed, it is a proactive and healthy way to unpack the things that are holding us back.

6. **Consider your role in this.** Just like in the example where my anticipation of the dentist was worse than the few minutes of actual pain, ask yourself if *your reaction* to the judgement is actually worse than the judgement itself. Who is causing you more suffering here – the hurler of judgement or yourself? Also, are you making it worse by complaining about it to others who then reinforce your pain, or by going back to that email or social media post and reading it over and over again and following the comments that come after?

7. **Reclaim mental equilibrium.** Meditation is the key to regaining mental equilibrium. Always.

If we give ourselves enough time, we may come to the conclusion that the judgement is not the problem; our wild monkey minds are the problem.

Going forward

The above list gives us some idea of how to deal with an immediate incidence of judgement that has triggered us into strong, disturbing emotions. But now let's think a bit bigger, more long term.

Ultimately, in Buddhist philosophy, everything that happens to us is a result of karma. In that sense, if judgement is coming your way, it is because at some point (in this life or any other) you have judged someone else. That's a sobering notion, but also, I think somewhat relieving.

Oh . . . I have been that person too.

As a judgemental twenty-something, I was probably not much different to a lot of younger people who are given to believing in ideals without having fully developed compassion and wisdom. But still, I am guilty of having judged others. Logically, why wouldn't other people now judge me? It should also give us hope, though, because each time we 'suffer', we are working off our karma. Buddhists say that karma 'ripens' at some point and makes itself evident in our life. The tricky thing is, we never know when that will be; however, if karma presents itself in my current life, it is giving me an opportunity to heal that moment; therefore, how I deal with that moment is vitally important, otherwise all I'm doing is creating more karma for myself to ripen again. I guess that's why the common wisdom says that 'stuff' keeps turning up in our life again and again until we fully deal with it. By mindfully making an effort to release our own judgements (not just the ones we speak out loud but the ones we think too), we are freeing ourselves from judgement coming back to us.

By accepting that I have been as judgemental as the person who is now judging me, I can begin to feel the tiny spark of compassion and forgiveness and then peace.

Journal Questions

1. Think of a time in your life when you felt judged by someone else. Does it feel as bad now as it did then? What did you learn about yourself during that situation?

2. Think of a time when you have judged someone else. What can you learn about yourself from that moment? Would you like to do it differently in the future? If so, how?

Seven

Yep, I'm Hearing You, But I Still Feel Guilty . . .

I get it. You're trying your best. One minute you've accepted that this is the way you need to eat, but then you see a cow with gorgeous big dark eyes and long lashes and you're pierced with guilt. First and foremost, we need to cultivate compassion for ourselves. If we lack that, we are more likely to lack it for others. Give yourself a break. Tell yourself that you are okay. Nurture yourself. Then embrace practical opportunities to extend compassion out to the animals too. In my experience, the best way to handle guilt is through action. Here's a list of twenty things you can do to proactively deal with disturbing emotions.

1. **Stop supporting horseracing.** Or dog racing, or any other kind of racing, for that matter. Greyhound rescuers have come a long way in educating the public on the horrors of dog racing, and it was a momentous moment when the entire greyhound racing industry was exposed a couple of years ago for the systemic cruelty involved in breeding, training, racing and the mass slaughter of dogs after their 'careers'. I was hopeful, for a moment, that the industry might be shut down for good, but it hasn't happened. I do, however, hold hope that the horseracing industry will also be suitably exposed.

   I can tell you firsthand of the many abuses of horseracing, the very *least* of which is the thousands of horses that are sent to slaughter each year for being too slow or because of injuries sustained from hard work long before they've even finished growing. Running a horse rescue charity, I've seen far more than I would have ever knowingly let myself see and once you've seen it you can't turn back. The problem, in part, is the amount of money involved with horseracing, the fact that the big names are usually extremely wealthy individuals who own companies and have their fingers in all sorts of political pies and the whole awful nightmare of 'tourism' and 'glamour' and 'celebrity' that goes with it (not to mention that public holiday for one race a year that nobody will want to let go of). As far as jumps races go (galloping horses over long distances and high-jumping obstacles, which frequently ends in deaths), there have been many parliamentary debates and reviews and senate inquiries into the industry, with the conclusion that there is no way to make this type of racing safe, and yet it still continues.

There is an entire book to be written about the devastating impact of horseracing. For now, please stop supporting it. If you want to gamble, there are plenty of other options that don't involve the lives of precious young animals that are used and abused in this industry. (And yes, I know there are always exceptions, but it isn't enough, not by far.)

2. **Sponsor a farm animal.** We currently sponsor three cows. We've long wanted to rescue some calves and have them on our property, but wisdom tells us we really don't have the knowledge or facilities to do it well. Sponsoring is the next best option and I like to believe is a good thing to do karmically. An online search will help you locate a registered charity near you.

3. **Get active about animal welfare in the meat industry.** Sign all the petitions. There is so much

that needs to change about intensive farming practices, with chickens and pigs in particular. Also, lobby your supermarkets to stock only free-range and organic products. If you have a smaller store, such as a local IGA, you can probably speak with the manager directly. Otherwise, email or phone or look for petitions online.

4. **Put your money where your mouth is.** This is often the only real way to make change happen. Choose the highest level of ethically sourced animal products every time. Always choose local wherever possible.

5. **Rescue animals.** Adopt from shelters and rescue organisations wherever possible. Take the time to try to help wandering or lost dogs, keep them safe and reunite them with their families. Take in stray cats (if wisdom permits!). Pick up fallen and injured birds. Call local wildlife hotlines for trickier animals (like injured kangaroos, goannas or snakes).

6. **Become a wildlife carer.** I'm always in awe of wildlife carers. They work hard, for no money, and I'm guessing a lot of stress. But we need more of them. Wildlife caring really is a call to service. To find out more about what's involved, contact your local wildlife caring group. An online search should help, or you could ask your local veterinarian to point you in the right direction.

7. **Foster animals.** Lots of charities need foster carers for animals while they're waiting for adoption. I fostered several horses while running my charity and several of them came to stay for life. This is a tricky commitment where you'll be tested emotionally in order to let them go again, but one that is so important. Animals that live in foster care situations are so much less stressed and able to recover than those stuck in concrete kennels in noisy, chaotic pounds.

8. **Donate to charities.** There are many wonderful animal charities around and the only way they can

continue is with financial donations. Setting up a regular, small donation is a great way to automate your giving. Search online to find the nearest registered charities to you.

9. **Volunteer your time.** You don't have to have surplus cash or open your home to animals. Heaps of organisations need help fundraising, or with admin and marketing work, sometimes cleaning animal cages, or looking after animals. If you are a professional dog trainer or have natural horsemanship skills, your local animal charity would be delighted to have you offer your time. Acupuncturists, massage therapists, reiki practitioners, herbalists and chiropractors are also often welcome. In my experience, almost all rescue animals have at least a couple of physical or emotional kinks to work through.

10. **Deal with your plastics.** It might be hard to commit straightway to a one hundred per cent plastic-free life, but perhaps aim for three goals a week to reduce your plastic consumption.

11. **Prayer and death services.** There are numerous studies that show prayer works. Whatever your version of prayer is, it has an effect. In Buddhist philosophy, when any living creature dies, their soul goes to the bardo (the space between lives) for up to seven weeks, and during this time you can influence their future life. This is not dissimilar to the Catholic tradition of saying prayers for the deceased. There are specific things we can do for our loved ones after death including: dedicating actions of merit to our animal's fortunate rebirth; donating to charitable organisations in their name; and saying mantras, meditating and holding them close mentally and emotionally, continuously sending energy of good fortune. After Daisy's death, these kinds of actions brought me moments of peace and gave me something to do, which in itself can be a meditative, focusing and calming activity.

You can also do these things for someone else's animal. I have a list of actions I take for animals who belong to my friends or family after they pass away. It brings the person comfort, as well as adds to my service to animals, assisting them towards a higher rebirth. The act is one of deep mindfulness, which of course benefits myself too.

12. **Be kind to your own animals.** I know this sounds simplistic, but the way we treat our animals now conveys to them how they should be treated in the future. If we want them to have a higher rebirth, then we need to demonstrate to them what to look for in a future life. You can't hug them too much. You can't tell them too often that you love them and they are worthy of love. David Michie in his book *Buddhism for Pet Lovers* advocates showing them images of Buddha, letting them meditate with you and also hearing the prayers and chants, thereby imprinting their souls with knowledge of Buddhism. This wisdom will hopefully stay with them and guide them towards finding a loving teacher in a future life.

More than that, I strongly believe that all animals are connected in a big web of light, and while we may not be able to release the poor moon bear that is trapped in a rusty bile-farming cage right now, we can pour love into the whole web. Great reasons to love your animals just that bit more!

13. **Start a business or hobby that supports animals.** (Hey, as the saying goes, you might as well aim for the moon as you might just land on a star.) I'm not suggesting you quit your day job. What I am offering is an idea, a whimsy if you like, that could sit as a seed in your mind and heart and perhaps ripen one day into something bigger that has a flow-on effect for the benefit of animals. To be clear, I am not talking about businesses that *use animals to generate profit* in the way horseracing or meat production does, or circuses do. From what I've observed, when a business relies on animals to make profit, the animals mostly lose in the

end (with a few exceptions, including therapeutic services for animals).

But if you love animals and have a keen eye for photography, then helping to celebrate and share the love of animals through your photographs could be wonderful. Or if you're a keen baker, you might choose to use cruelty-free ingredients, sell your goods and donate a portion to animal charities. Or you might be crafty and love illustrating and create greeting cards with beautiful images of animals. Or perhaps you are a budding filmmaker and want to make documentaries about animals. Baking and craft activities are also great options to get kids involved, thereby teaching them to appreciate animals from a young age. If you sit with the intention long enough, the right idea will come to you, I'm sure.

14. **Practise bodhicitta.** Bodhicitta is the spontaneous desire to help everyone achieve enlightenment (not just yourself). In doing so, we want the rest

of the world to reach enlightenment because we feel compassion for everyone and know that all benefit when we reach enlightenment together. In practice, what this means is that you can devote almost anything to the enlightenment of yourself and animals. Every time you feed your animals, brush them, care for them and love them, you can mentally dedicate that moment to the world's enlightenment.

15. **Moments of love.** There was a time when Hubby and I were preparing to rescue some calves. To research this, I went to the next local cattle sale, which happened each month, an hour's drive from our place.

It was brutal. There were two young calves, both in a pen on their own, clearly too young to be off their mothers. The calves had scouring diarrhoea and huge eyes, mooing desperately to be heard above the cacophony of louder bellows from full-grown cattle. As I was standing there watching them, a man in jeans, boots and a cowboy hat came to the pen and pulled each of them out by the tail, shoved them down a walkway, up a ramp and into the back of a small truck. One of the calves fell onto its knees then struggled to get up again. The man slammed the door and moved away, ignoring my shocked face.

I went to the side of the truck where the calves were panting and mooing. One stopped and stared at me with its terrified eyes – something I will never forget. I fought back tears and spoke to it. 'You are a good cow. You did nothing wrong. You deserve better than this. You are a good cow.'

Thinking back to that day, it still makes me cry. But I also believe in that one moment when the calf and I stood connected, my love for him went somewhere into his mind and lodged itself there. The thing is, we never know what moments in life stay with a soul, which acts of kindness, which acts of compassion, which moments of connection.

Many of us would have had 'a moment' that transformed us in some way, or experienced someone's support in a difficult moment that made it so much easier to bear. (If you've had a rough exit out of anaesthetic after an operation, you may well know how much the nurse's voice and gentle touch helped you in that time.)

I don't think there's any reason to believe an animal would be different. At the very least, there's nothing to lose if we offer our love in a moment of suffering, right? I've done it with many horses at auctions, the ones I couldn't save. I want them to feel at least a tiny bit of love before they die. So, I will continue to tell animals that they are good and kind and wise and that they deserve all good things.

16. **Lobby your wholefood stores.** Organic stores seem like they should be a safe place to purchase ethical products and for the most part that's true. But recently I bought some handwash in my local

wholefood store, only to bring it home to note with dismay that it included palm oil in the ingredients. I emailed the store to let them know that I hoped in the future they would reconsider stocking products that contained palm oil. Commercial enterprises stock what consumers want, it's as simple as that. Use your voice to let them know.

17. **Be a rubbish warrior.** This is a step further than just dealing with your own plastic problem. Litter hurts our wildlife and aquatic animals, filling their bellies with plastics, choking them, trapping them, and leaving them to die slow and painful deaths. You could choose a strip of your local beach or bushland or even the street outside your house to regularly remove rubbish, saving it from ending up in the water or in animals' guts or around their necks. Our planet is suffocating in waste. Don't underestimate your contribution here.

18. **Find your bottom line.** This is a powerful activity in mindfulness. If you know you need to eat some

meat to stay healthy, work to find your bottom line. That is, keep a food diary to figure out how much you really need to eat. You might even find you aren't eating as much as you thought you were. Conversely, you might see you're eating more than you thought. Knowledge is power and keeping records of food is empowering data. Do you need to eat meat every day, three times a week, once a week, twice a fortnight, or twice a month? Knowing your numbers can help you find peace.

19. **Plant and protect native trees (or donate to an organisation that can do this for you).** Despite what sensationalist headlines would like to tell you, cats are not the number-one killer of our wildlife. The main destroyer of our wildlife populations in this country is land clearing. That's not a politically popular thing to say, though; it's easier and stirs up more online furore (more clicks! more likes! more shares!) to spread cat hatred. To be clear, I acknowledge that both cats *and dogs* pose

huge threats to our wildlife. That's why our cats stay indoors all the time and our dogs are always inside at night. But deforestation is a far bigger problem, if only because once land is cleared it takes decades to replace and it can never be replenished the same way as it was before, even if we realised our terrible error and tried to rectify it.

It's really very simple. Native animals need native forests in which to live and especially so in corridors (connected tracts of land). When land is fragmented, they are at risk of attack by dogs, and injury and death by car accidents. Stress causes them to get ill.

These problems can extend beyond the 'simple' loss of species. Take the example of cassowaries, that huge bird of the northern Queensland Daintree Rainforest, which appears a bit like an emu and has a fierce-looking horn on its head. The cassowary is listed nationally as an endangered bird and while this is sad enough in itself, there is also a more significant issue. Cassowaries are known as the 'gardeners' of the forests. They eat forest fruits, digest the flesh and then pass out the seeds, which germinate and grow, thereby constantly replanting tree species throughout the forest. Sometimes, the seeds they eat are so big that they are the only animal large enough to swallow and pass them on. Without cassowaries tending our precious rainforest, the consequences could be dire and spread to more animal species that rely on the trees that cassowaries distribute.

I have been regenerating a tract of land on our property predominantly with natives and some smaller exotic flowers (like lavender, which I just can't seem to do without). Native plants are sensible choices, because they are adapted to your area so they are incredibly hardy and water-wise, they attract native birds and wildlife, which is delightful and helps provide food for them when their choices are diminishing, and are perfect for lazy gardeners who don't want to do much maintenance.

We also have a tradition of buying a native tree every Christmas and planting it on the property. If we did that and nothing else, we would have planted a good fifty trees in our lifetime. If you live in an apartment or without a suitable yard, perhaps you could support a local revegetation project instead.

One of my favourite charities is the Australian Koala Foundation. I make it a habit to donate money for their koala food tree planting program every time I get royalties, which has the added benefit of enhancing my feelings of gratitude for my career and for everyone who buys one of my books. Automating an action such as planting a native tree each year at Christmas or donating to an organisation for tree planting at a certain time helps ensure you keep track of your goodwill actions.

20. **Live by example.** I know it can be really frustrating, and even painful, to feel we are surrounded by people who 'just don't get it'. I think, though, that His Holiness the Dalai Lama and Thich Nhat Hanh are fabulous proof that you can live by example and others will follow. Ranting at people, shaming them or guilt-tripping them tends to push them away, rather than bring them closer. Buddhists aren't in the business of converting; we're in the business of living by example. Be the light that dispels the darkness and draw others to your flame of hope.

Practical Challenge

Choose three things from the list of twenty things you can do and organise them today.

In a month's time, pause and think about what you've achieved in the past four weeks – how have these commitments helped you to reconcile your thoughts with your actions? Have you noticed any changes in yourself, such as in your levels of optimism, joy or peace? Has anyone else been inspired by your actions? Have there been any flow-on effects, such as meeting new friends, saving money or less waste leaving your home?

Eight

The Gift of Impermanence

Everything changes.

Buddhists and psychologists alike would tell us that the sooner we come to terms with the nature of impermanence, the happier we'll be. Just as wisdom and compassion are two well-matched dance partners, so too are attachment and impermanence. The more we cling to attachments, the more we suffer when they inevitably change.

The animals in our lives can be master teachers of this soft shoe shuffle between attachment and impermanence. Attached to that lovely leather couch? *Pfft.* It will be wrecked by your animals' claws in a matter of days. Attached to the idea of a perfect afternoon tea party in the garden? A dog like Daisy will ensure she takes herself off for a walk to roll in manure before barrelling gleefully up the hill and throwing herself into the lap of your most dog-adverse, pristinely dressed-in-white guest. Attached to your favourite pair of shoes? Whoops, the puppy just destroyed them.

Daisy entered my life somewhat like an illusion-shattering golden cannonball barrelling through my home and heart, changing it forever. Hubby and I had been dating for six months when he decided to *surprise me* with an eight-week-old golden retriever. (Yes, he is now well aware that you should never buy a dog as a surprise gift for anyone.) At the time, I was living with my sister and her two cats in a small two-bedroom house that had no fences around the yard. The result was a gigantic upheaval and a whole lot of upset for everyone involved. Future Hubby and I had to rapidly find a place to live together on acreage so I could get out of my sister's space, raise this puppy properly and move my horse Hercules out of agistment and into my backyard. Fortunately, the result was one that ended in marriage for us and a growing menagerie of animals, but just about every aspect of my life – personal, housing, financial, work, relationships, dreams – was affected or broken down. It was intensely stressful. That was the power of my experience with Daisy dog, a masterclass in impermanence, except I didn't have enough knowledge at the time to understand that and, sadly, I didn't see her death coming almost twelve years later because I simply wouldn't allow myself to even truly contemplate it.

Animals don't live as long as we do and therefore die so much sooner than we expect them to. Their deaths are very real reminders to us of the swift passage of time and the all-too-real notion that anyone at any moment can be taken away. A grieving heart can do one of two things – shut down and hide away from future pain or be broken open into something bigger than it was before. If we let it, the power of grief will make us more sensitive to others' pain, more compassionate to the moment in front of us, more determined to help others.

When an animal of mine dies I grieve. It's not always the same, because my relationship with every one of them is different. Each time, I look around at the extent of our animal family and I take stock of how often I'll have to say goodbye and I have a short-lived tantrum because I simply don't want to feel this pain over and over again. Why have I done this to myself? Why would I knowingly put myself in the path of so much grief? I think, in part, it is because of impermanence. It is knowing that this awful pain will too one day lessen and ease and change. The loss of Daisy threatened to completely undo me. But then,

I knew that there would be a moment in the future when I didn't feel quite as bad as I did right at that moment. Even if I sat in that pain for six months or twelve months, I would never have traded it for the years I'd had her to bring joy into my life. It had been worth it, absolutely.

The passing of an animal such as a cat or dog is often so tied up with an era of time. My cat Jasmine was eighteen when she died and I'd had her through my university years, several failed relationships and careers, unemployment, surgeries, career-forging years, new love, marriage and a child. She'd sat on my lap at the computer while I'd written university assignments through to job applications, multiple failed novels and finally bestselling novels. She'd borne witness to all of those moments.

Daisy was there for the 'first big era' of my life with Hubby, from dating through marriage, four homes, dozens of animals, multiple businesses and lifestyles, and a miscarriage, pregnancy and then birth of our son, and the way she had lovingly guarded him as a baby and 'raised' him through his first five-and-a-half years of life. It was the loss of all of it that hurt but it was also the hard, cold reminder that huge parts of our life were now over, drifting away, constantly. Animals remind us of our own mortality and the mortality of those around us. Hopefully, the grief makes us better people because we want to be more present, more considerate, more loving of the ones we have left.

Our bodies and impermanence

Our bodies are changing. The person you are right now is literally not the same person you were a minute ago, because inside your body cells are transforming all the time – digesting, generating, communicating, transporting, living and dying. Mostly, we tend to think of our bodies as getting 'worse' through the process of ageing. But labelling something as 'worse' is a judgement that isn't helpful. It is different, yes.

But worse? Not necessarily. What about those times your body heals an injury, or a sore, or an illness? If you paused time at the moment you were in hospital or the moment you couldn't work because of illness it would seem bleak. But nothing is permanent. Something is always changing, even if it is your thoughts, your feelings or your level of compassion towards yourself or others. Often, our bodies even get better with age in more obvious ways.

My Shetland pony Sparky is known in our house as 'the phoenix'. Sparky is one of my rescues and is approximately thirty years old, though no one can tell for sure. I've had him for nine years now and he's been plagued by issues from day one, arriving at our place in spectacular form with a fever of forty-two degrees and difficulty breathing. This was back in 2010 when there wasn't yet a vaccine for Hendra virus (an Australian virus that infects horses, leading to death, and which may also be passed to humans and has led to deaths in some of those people too).

The equine community was alarmed at the cases popping up around the country and the frightening number of people who had contracted the illness from their horse. Sparky's symptoms triggered a full-on 'bio suit' visit from the vet and his blood had to be sent away to the Department of Primary Industries while our place was quarantined. Fortunately, he did not have Hendra virus but rather some form of respiratory illness, which happened to be the first of many.

Over the years, we added all sorts of diagnoses to his list, including Cushing's Disease (which is common in old horses and causes a litany of flow-on conditions, including the serious and painful hoof condition laminitis, which is reported to be the second-biggest killer of horses after colic), as well as airway disease (he now has his own asthma medication and spacer for when he has an attack), partial deafness and diabetes. He's on two types of medication every day, and the vet has been called out frequently in the middle of the night for what we were convinced would be his last night on earth. On one visit, Sparky collapsed at the vet's feet not just once, but *twice*. So many times we called the vet convinced euthanasia was the only option. But Sparky never gave us 'the look' – even when he was lying on the ground and refusing to eat! – but rather shows a fierce, stubborn determination to battle on.

Finally, we found some key ways to improve Sparky's health and he seems to have regenerated. So much so that several of my other horses are now frightened of him, and recently he even tried to bolt through the gate to enter the house yard. When I firmly shooed him away, he turned his rump to me and started to lift both back legs to kick me in a stunning display of a temper tantrum before he thought better of it. My response was to grin with glee and shout to Hubby. 'Did you see that!?' It was proof at just how far Sparky had come, the power of impermanence manifest in his bounding good health.

When Daisy died suddenly, several people shook their heads in disbelief and said, 'But Sparky's still here!' He'd been the one who was 'supposed' to go first. I'm convinced he'll outlive every single animal in our house.

My own body is better now than it was thirteen years ago, when I had chronic fatigue syndrome. At one point, I had terrible plantar fasciitis (severe inflammation of the feet) for eighteen months, having to tape my feet every day to walk, only to have the condition completely gone now. My tailbone was damaged during the birth of my child and I lived with agony for another nine months, not being able to sit for long (a great challenge if you have a sedentary job like a writer and live in the country where it's an hour's drive to a supermarket). I'd all but given up on recovering when I found a good doctor who administered some injections in just the right spot and fixed it. There was also the time I sprained my wrist and had it constantly braced for about six months until it got better. Last year, I joined a gym and lifted weights three times a week for a year. It didn't give me a body builder's physique, but I could lift more weight at the end of that year than I could at the start. I could list many more of these examples and I'm sure if you think about it you can recall these types of situations in your own life too, noting that our bodies are constantly changing and, sometimes, even for the better.

Food and impermanence

Once you've identified all the ways your body has improved over the years, you might come to the happy conclusion that it is *possible* that the type of food your body wants right now may not *always* be the type of food it wants. It is possible that one day, a vegetarian or vegan diet may actually align with your wishes. It also may not. This is where our understanding of attachment and impermanence comes in. The more we can let go of ideals and belief systems about what should be, the more we allow the flow of change (impermanence) to run through our bodies and minds. I will always continue to work with gut-healing methods (one of the best, so they say, is bone broths), but I do it because I want to be healthy. If, by some miracle, that means one day I am able to eat vegetable protein again, that will be a happy day, but I am no longer attached to that outcome.

Beyond this, there are likely all sorts of other changes to the meat industry and protein industries that are still coming along that might also open new doors for us. 'Clean meat' is meat that has been grown in a laboratory from stem cells and has us wondering if this is the humane future of animal protein consumption. I'm not sure how I feel about that yet, but I am heartened by people's efforts to think a little differently about meat sources.

Cricket protein, and insect protein in general, has been getting more attention as a sustainable source of animal protein. (Before it went bankrupt, the Mars One project included plans for the growing of insects as a food source for its future citizens on Mars.) I'm seeing insect protein more and more in wholefood stores as snacks and biscuits. This is one of those Middle Way questions you would have to assess for yourself – it obviously takes many more individual insect lives to create as much protein as the life of one cow, but it is far more environmentally friendly. Which is 'worse'? Which option is best for you and your circumstances? Only you can decide that.

Closer to home, hemp seeds were finally approved as a food in Australia late 2017 and there has been a boom in hemp products on the shelf. It is being touted as THE next big protein miracle for plant-based diets because by weight hemp seeds provide roughly the same amount of protein as beef or lamb. Win! Except that, for me, while I enjoy the taste and am more than happy to eat them, they also make me sick and give me reflux. But you might be compatible with them. Lucky you!

If it's not hemp seeds, it could be something else. While I haven't quantified it, our food choices (at least, here in Australia) seem to be diversifying, which means we have more and more chances to find the foods that work for our body. What is on food shelves today is not what was there fifteen years ago – impermanence. I turned gluten-free in 1991 and back then almost no one had even heard of gluten, and you had to make every single thing from scratch because gluten-free food didn't come with convenience. These days, there is a gluten-free alternative to almost everything and menus are full of options. Even going back around ten years, it seemed nearly all vegetarian products were full of soy. These days, there is a huge range of vegetarian foods that are free of soy and include amazing beans, for example. Food is changing, all the time. (Remember, it was only in recent memory that coconut went from being a 'bad fat' to being the huge industry it is today.) That means we simply don't know what's around the corner.

Accept where you're at right now, but be open to the idea that it might not always be this way and could even work in your favour.

To accept impermanence is to live in harmony with the flow of life. Rigid ideals and labels lock us into non-acceptance of what is. To approach each moment mindfully – to question, 'What is right for me in this particular instance?' – takes patience and compassion and practice. It is to understand that what is right in this moment may not be right in the next, and to be willing to be okay with that.

How you feel about food today might not be the same as how you feel about it next year, next week, or even tomorrow. If you've binged on ice-cream and feel hideously guilty, know that feeling will pass. If you've eaten meat for the fifth day in a row and shame is creeping up your body, that feeling will pass too. This day will end and will be fresh again tomorrow. That's the beauty of this wonderful, complicated life we're living.

Journal Questions

1. Think back over your life. In what ways has your body improved and changed over the years?

2. In what ways have you noticed food change over the past twenty years? Ten years? Five years? What about the food you see in cafes and restaurants and on supermarket shelves? Do you make different choices now because of these changes?

3. Have you ever suffered a loss that has changed the way you looked at the world?

4. If you knew today was going to be your last day on earth, what would you do? Who would you speak to? What would you say?

Practical Challenge

Go and do one of those things you said you would do on your last day on earth. Afterwards, reflect on how you felt while doing it. Would you like to do that more often? If so, how could you include more of that in your life?

Nine

Ethical Choices and
My Favourite Resources

Pet food choices

In 2018, we finally saw a senate inquiry into pet food in Australia. About time!

When I ran my horse rescue charity, my husband and I did a lot of research into pet food, mostly because we knew that slaughtered horses are used as an ingredient (they don't call the slaughterman who buys horses at auction 'the dogger' for nothing) and we wanted to get more information. Hubby phoned every dog food company in Australia. With the exception of one brand, they all told him verbally that they did not use horse meat but refused to put it in writing. Now, I'm not going to argue that using horse meat is any 'worse' than using any other meat, but this is merely one example of the fact that we really have no idea what is in commercial pet food. The thing with pet food is that the ingredient labelling laws are scant. Most of the 'standards' are voluntary and (at the time of writing) the industry as a whole is self-regulating.

Dog deaths have been associated with pet food in the past. All manner of toxins (including melamine, plastics and metals), colours, fillers, preservatives (well above safety levels) and additives have been found in commercial pet food. There has been a surge in the number of grain-free diets on the market, as people have slowly realised that packing pet food with wheat, corn, rye and various starches does nothing to enhance a dog or cat's life and may even be harmful. But recently, veterinarians in the USA launched an investigation into grain-free diets (which are typically high in chickpeas, lentils and other legumes) because they were suspicious these foods were contributing to cardiomyopathy (chronic disease of the heart) in dogs. The same issues with legumes also apply to vegan dog and cat food, which relies on those same plant proteins. From our experience, when we changed over our cats to a grain-free diet *all* of them got urinary crystals (potentially deadly in cats) and they now have to live on special urinary health biscuits to stop repeat episodes.

Many years ago, pet food contained such small amounts of actual red meat that dogs and cats became deficient in taurine, an amino acid and important component to protect their heart, eyes and nervous system and they began to die. As a result, pet food companies had to start adding taurine into their nutrient-deficient food. You may still find commercial pet food on the market with 'added taurine' to catch your eye.

The majority of commercial pet food comes from animals not deemed fit for human consumption – that means, diseased, cancerous, contaminated, rotting, as well as meat that has been rendered. Look that one up, if you dare. You won't want to buy anything rendered ever again. While you're at it, you might want to look up how 'raw hide' products are made. You probably won't ever buy them again, either. (They're also responsible for dog deaths from contamination and intestinal blockages . . . amazing what they don't tell you, isn't it?) Also, you might want to do a search on 'pet food recalls' and see how long the list is. It's scary.

Do we really want our beloved animals eating this stuff? Of course not. We love our animals and want them to live long and healthy lives. As well, the majority of pet food comes from factory-farmed or lot-fed animals, which means those animals have suffered unnecessarily in the high-density world of meat production.

From an ethical perspective, we should be most concerned with where our pet food comes from. The only way you can do this is to carefully choose foods yourself. Go for human-grade foods wherever you can, and ones you know are organic and free range. By being mindful of your pet food choices, you minimise your impact on the suffering of animals everywhere (as well as the environment) and invest your money where your ethics lie.

These days, there are lots of books and websites out there to teach you how to feed your cats and dogs raw food diets (which is what they are biologically evolved to eat). If you're new to these raw food diets, you might feel nervous about this, which is understandable given the multi-billion-dollar power of pet food advertising that convinces you that you couldn't possibly provide everything your animal needs. But if you can feed yourself and your family – if you learned to feed a baby, then a toddler, then a child – you can feed your pets, and you can do it knowing you're not accidentally poisoning them with hidden chemicals and toxins and you're choosing the most compassionate options available.

Yes, it takes more thought to begin with, but once you're in the swing of it, it will be just the same as preparing your other meals. Yes, it will cost more. There's a reason for that – you're buying actual food! We know that poor diets lead to poor health. For my money, I'd rather be spending more each week to know my animals are eating the best food I can manage now, rather than spending thousands trying to fix their ill health later, or saying goodbye for good because they're too sick to save.

Of course, you will have to find your Middle Way. For us, it's often a combination of a raw-food diet plus the best possible pre-prepared dog food we can find. At the moment, we are loving ZiwiPeak dog food (www.ziwipets.com), which comes from

New Zealand and includes no grains, rendered products or artificial additives and comes only from certified free-range animals. They also use human-grade meats. (I emailed them to confirm this, which they did in writing.)

Food choices
Pork

Pork is one food I will never ever touch. The reason for this is that pigs suffer horribly in intensive farming practices – and most pork products on the shelf are from intensive farming. Truly, awful things happen to pigs. You can research 'sow stalls' to get just a small sense of the horrors these incredibly intelligent beings endure for your bacon.

Shark/Flake/Shark Fin

Sharks suffer cruel mutilations and deaths in their harvest. As well, sharks are apex predators in the ocean. Apex predators, the top predators of a food chain, are crucial to the healthy functioning of an entire ecosystem and their removal can have long-lasting and potentially catastrophic effects. Crocodiles are also apex predators, with important management roles in healthy waterways. I would never eat any of these products.

Chicken/eggs

I can't count the number of times I have heard someone say, 'Chickens are stupid.' I beg to differ. We keep our own chickens and I assure you they are far from stupid. One of our girls, named Mama Chicken by our son, quickly sorted out our little dog, Molly, who likes to fancy herself as a bit of chicken chaser (she is part terrier). Mama Chicken sized her up and immediately adopted the strategy of playing dead whenever Molly tried to chase her around.

She is so good at this that one day I looked out the window to see Mama Chicken on the ground, flat on her chest, her wings hanging lifelessly at odd angles, her head turned to the side, her mouth open and her eyes glassy. Molly was standing over her. I rushed out, furious with Molly, reached Mama Chicken's side and noted her tongue was also hanging out. She was gone, for sure.

I bent down to lift her up, preparing to bury her, when she snapped to attention at my touch, fluffed her feathers and continued on her way, strutting her stuff past a very confused Molly and me.

Mama Chicken lets herself out of the yard daily by climbing to the roof of the chook house and flying over the fence to the house yard, where she free ranges through the day and then takes herself back to bed at night. But one afternoon, darkness was nearly complete and she was at the back door to the kitchen, murmuring at me for attention, and walking side to side. 'Mama Chicken, go to bed,' I said, busily making dinner. But she didn't go.

'Why's Mama Chicken here?' Hubby said.

'I don't know.' We both stood and stared at her a moment. Then a very clear thought popped into my head. 'I bet they've run out of water.'

Sure enough, Hubby went down and the water supply had tipped over and was bone dry. Mama Chicken had come to the door to tell us and she wasn't going home until we'd fixed it.

Another of our chickens, Miss Candyhooves, a black Australorp, had an entirely different way of fending off Molly when she wanted to chase her. Candyhooves would run as fast as she could and make the most incredible hullabaloo that would send us bolting outside and chasing them around trying to rescue her, convinced she was dying a terrible death. In reality, noise was her strategy. She used it to shock and disorient the dog, who likely couldn't think straight through the dreadful din and simply walked away.

Chook lovers everywhere will tell you that a chicken can be the most amazing friend, who will follow you around, talk to you, sit on you and join you in the house if you'll let her. Each one has a totally unique personality and individual likes and dislikes. They have feelings. They make friends in their flock. They love the sun, they love to bathe in the dust, and they love a quiet, dark, nurturing space to lay their eggs in private. They deserve an awful lot better than a short, brutal, fluorescent-lit, noisy, wire-caged factory farmed life. Always choose organic, as by definition it is also free-range. Better yet, keep your own chooks. They really add joy to your life, as well as fertiliser for your garden, and provide good natural pest control, as they eat bugs.

Chocolate

Oh my, chocolate is a minefield of ethical choices. Whole books are written covering these issues, so I can only touch on it here. Most chocolate you find on the supermarket shelf is cheap because it exploits the farmers who work for it. Cacao is a cash crop, grown in a narrow band in rainforests either side of the equator, in countries where few, if any, labour laws exist to protect workers. The world being as it is, large corporations look for ways to upscale their investments in these crops on the other side of the world, far from where their head offices are. That means, you guessed it, they clear rainforests (which is the natural habit of the cacao tree) in order to plant more trees.

Aside from the obvious issues of destroying precious rainforests (you know, the things that give us oxygen), land clearing kills loads of animals in the process. Cacao trees evolved to thrive under the canopy of taller rainforest trees. To counter this, company executives decided to propagate new varieties of trees that could survive the extra sunlight and could grow faster to produce more beans. But problems ensued, including the fact that these trees needed more water than could be sustainably replenished, they didn't live as long, and have a lower resistance to pests. More pests naturally result in more pesticides and traps, which leads to animal deaths, which is bad for our karma. And we're not just talking insects here. Lots of mammals, like squirrels and monkeys, hang around cacao trees too.

You have to choose chocolate carefully. Look for brands that give you detailed explanations of what the business is doing to support the rainforest environment and also the workers, rather than just stamping the label with some sort of supposedly rainforest-friendly logo. Search for brands that are handcrafted and made on site in the country of origin, rather than having beans shipped halfway around the world to be made into chocolate before being shipped halfway around the world again to sell to you. Chocolate would have to have some of the biggest food miles on the planet.

Daintree Estates (www.daintreeestates.com.au) is a chocolate company that grows their cacao in Australia. They farm their cacao trees in Mossman, north of Cairns, which happens to fall in the narrow band either side of the equator that provides the right climate for the beans. I visited one of their farms while researching my novel, *The Chocolate Promise*. I can attest that their chocolate is delicious and, though it might not be organic, at the very least they are utilising existing farms (in the case of the one I visited, it was a sugarcane farm) rather than cutting down rainforest, paying workers Australian labour awards, and keeping the food miles down.

Coffee

Coffee is also a rainforest plant grown either side of the equator and a cash crop, so has near-identical issues to chocolate. As always, do your research carefully to see where exactly your money is going, favour organic sources where possible, and have a look for locally grown beans if you can find them. There are more than thirty coffee growers in Australia you could choose to support. Simply search online for 'coffee growers Australia' and you will find them.

Tea

If you're a teabag user, I'm sorry to be the bearer of bad news but your teabag more than likely contains plastic. Yes, you read that correctly. Plastic threads are used to reinforce the teabag so that it doesn't fall apart in the boiling water. Makes sense now you think about it, doesn't it? But that means *your tea is brewing in plastic water*! Choose loose-leaf tea and take the opportunity to enjoy a moment of mindfulness (or longer, if you'd like to follow Thich Nhat Hanh's example), or look for teabags that are plastic-free or one-hundred per cent compostable. (Side note: the term 'biodegradable' doesn't necessarily mean compostable. Something labelled biodegradable still might take five or more years to break down, which is too long.) For more information on this, do an online search for 'teabags plastic' and you'll uncover a wealth of information on this topic.

If making a pot of tea just seems too hard, you can also buy cotton drawstring teabags (search online for these) that you can fill with your favourite organic herbs and teas and make your cup of tea that way.

Sushi

I love sushi and I savour taking my young son out on 'sushi dates'. However, I am deeply disturbed by the amount of plastic packaging that generally comes with it, which you might only use for a couple of minutes (or seconds!) by the time it takes to walk to a seat to eat it, not to mention all those plastic fish-shaped soy sauce containers and ginger and wasabi packets. Here are a few ways I've managed to reduce my sushi impact.

○ Eat in and really enjoy yourself. Use the phrase 'mindfulness with miso', if it helps you to remember. My son loves the sushi train and he'll often experiment with food he wouldn't otherwise touch if I handed it to him out of a packet. Also, the food is far fresher than you find in the takeaway because the chefs are making it right there in front of you. As well, I've found a disturbing trend in the pre-packaged sushi rolls (such as what you'd find in petrol stations, supermarkets or takeaway food stalls) to contain MSG (monosodium gluta-mate, labelled as flavour enhancer 621), which is listed on the ingredients on the packet. MSG gives me migraines. No, thank you.

○ Take your own container. Like many parents, we sometimes struggle with the school lunch run and sushi is usually our solution, which we can pick up on the way. These days, we carry our son's lunchbox to the counter and ask them to put it straight into the box. We also ask for no takeaway soy sauce.

○ Carry your own paper bags around. You can buy lunch bags easily enough, or even plain paper bags from the newsagent, and stuff a couple in your bag or pocket. If you're taking away, hand over the bag and ask for the sushi rolls to go in there.

○ As a last resort, simply ask them to put the sushi rolls in a paper towel.

As far as animal welfare goes, it's almost guaranteed that the animal products used in sushi are not organic or free range. The good news, though, is there are a lot of vegetarian sushi options on offer.

Fresh Box (www.freshbox.com.au)
This is where we get our fresh fruit and vegetables from. If you're on the Sunshine Coast in Queensland, you're in luck! If not, I encourage you to do an online search to find a similar organisation near you.

Tree, plastic and humanitarian heroes
Who Gives a Crap (www.whogivesacrap.org)
This organisation makes toilet paper from one hundred per cent recycled materials, uses cardboard boxes to package their products, delivers straight

to your door and gives *fifty per cent* of their profits to charities that specialise in water, sanitation and hygiene projects in impoverished communities around the world. What's not to love? They also make paper towels and tissues.

We have a recurring order set up, so all our paper needs arrive every eight weeks. By using these products, we know we've achieved our goal of plastic reduction, we save a heap of water, trees and energy, and we're helping the roughly forty per cent of the world's population (seriously!) who don't have access to proper sanitation (and that includes the children who die every few seconds from preventable diseases such as those attributed to lack of adequate hygiene).

If you want to go a bit more luxe, they even have products made from bamboo fibre! Who Gives a Crap have websites dedicated to Australia, the USA and the UK.

Books

Thich Nhat Hanh

The Miracle of Mindfulness: An Introduction to the Practice of Meditation

No Death, No Fear: Comforting Wisdom for Life

Living Buddha, Living Christ

Basically, anything Thich Nhat Hanh writes is eloquent, powerful and deeply stirring.

His Holiness the Dalai Lama

The Art of Happiness: A Handbook for Living

Healing Anger: The Power of Patience from a Buddhist Perspective

Meshel Laurie

Buddhism for the Unbelievably Busy

Buddhism for Break-ups

David Michie

*Buddhism for Pet Lovers: Supporting Our Closest
Companions Through Life and Death*

Eckhart Tolle

*The Power of Now: A Guide to Spiritual
Enlightenment*

Sarah Wilson

*First, We Make the Beast Beautiful: A New Story
About Anxiety*

Will McCallum

*How to Give Up Plastic: A Guide to Changing the
World, One Plastic Bottle at a Time*

Anita Vandyke

A Zero Waste Life in Thirty Days

189

Online

Calm (meditation app)

Headspace (meditation app)

Smiling Mind (meditation app, including kids' meditations)

The Chopra Center (www.chopracentermeditation. com) Deepak Chopra and Oprah Winfrey regularly offer free 21-day meditation courses.

Becoming Minimalist (www.becomingminimalist. com), including the associated 12-week Uncluttered course.

I did the 12-week decluttering course and loved it so much. Embracing minimalism doesn't mean living like a monk, but it does mean freeing yourself of many disturbing thoughts about 'stuff' and making wise choices that help our planet (thereby saving lives and earning yourself good karma). If you're serious about getting rid of plastics in your life, this is a great place to start. If making any change seems too hard, this is also a great place to start as you are taken through each room step by step and the associated Facebook group for your cohort of declutterers is a good support system. It will bring mindful consumerism to the forefront of your habits.

Hashtags
#meatfreemonday
#plasticfreefriday
#breakfreefromplastic
#nuptothecup

Ashley Jubinville (www.thekitchencoach.com)
Ashely teaches you how to reset your kitchen and to live well via plant-based foods and minimise food waste. Courses are accessible online.

Some of My Favourite Charities

The Australian Koala Foundation
(www.savethekoala.com)
Campaigning for the legislation of a Koala Protection Act, education and tree planting.

The Smith Family (www.thesmithfamily.com.au)
Helping disadvantaged children get the most out of their education.

Story Dogs (www.storydogs.org.au)
Improving children's literacy outcomes via the non-judgemental support of canine reading friends in the classroom.

RSPCA (www.rspca.org.au)
The peak national body for the protection of animals in Australia and the only animal charity with legal powers. To some extent, they campaign for better laws

for farmed animals too. They have an awfully difficult job to contend with.

Animals Australia (www.animalsaustralia.org)
Campaigning and advocacy for animals, particularly farm animals, animals involved in the meat industry and in the racing industries.

4ocean (www.4ocean.com)
Removing plastic from the ocean.

Greenpeace (www.greenpeace.org)
Worldwide organisation campaigning for environmental sustainability across all sectors.

Rainforest Rescue (www.rainforestrescue.org.au)
All things rainforest! Buying land, protecting land, rehabilitation, education, campaigns in Australia and internationally.

Ten

I Have
the Answer

Remember at the start of the book I said that I kept a journal for years, trying to find the answer to why my body wants meat while my spirit doesn't, but after years of struggling to work it out the answer was that I had no idea? Well, from a Buddhist perspective, having no idea is a marvellous opportunity, as we are encouraged to consider everything from a place of 'emptiness'. In putting my journal away, I released myself from my mental struggle and left the door open to see what turned up.

I think now, after all these years, I finally know the answer as to my predicament. I know why I've had this great 'misalignment' of values to grapple with through life. I *think* I know the answer, anyway, as much as we can ever know anything within the great flow of life's impermanence. For me, this whole journey of learning to reconcile these two halves of myself comes down to this.

I am a better person now for having had to work this out.

Learning to accept that things are rarely black and white, that labels are only ever marginally useful, if at all, and fully accepting that life involves suffering and our job is to work out how to find peace within that, has made me a far more compassionate person than I would have been if I'd been able to rigidly embrace the ideals I wanted to be true. I've had to accept that if I can't even make *myself* do what I believed to be *right*, then I couldn't possibly demand that of others, either.

It's so easy to judge people without knowing their stories.

A friend of mine is deaf in one ear and said she was at a noisy dinner talking to the person on her right for most of the night until the woman on her left had a go at her for constantly ignoring her when she spoke. My friend had to explain that, actually, she can't hear from that ear and had no idea the woman had been trying to speak to her.

It's so easy to judge the person who drives their car into work every day, contributing all those fossil fuels into the atmosphere, rather than easily catching the train, without knowing that they have chronic fatigue syndrome and the mere act of having to walk up the stairs is too much for them and they have to conserve every ounce of energy they can.

It's so easy to judge the abattoir workers until you realise they are refugees who can't speak English very well and the only way they can feed their family is to take the jobs that no one else wants, even if it's illegal for the company to use them for cheap labour.

It's so easy to judge the person who never makes eye contact and launches into conversations about abstract technical things without trying to engage you in conversation until you understand they have Asperger's syndrome and communicating is difficult (even painful) for them.

It's so easy to judge the person who pulled their car out in front of you in your lane of traffic, completely unaware you were there, and you had to slam on the brakes, angry, but you simply don't know that they just received a terrible medical diagnosis and their whole world just fell apart.

It's so easy to judge the animal lover for eating meat.

It's just so easy to judge.

All too easy.

Having to find compassion for myself means

that I understand I'm not perfect. I'm not the way I thought I would be. I make mistakes. I behave badly sometimes. I say the wrong things sometimes (or even frequently). But I am trying so damn hard to get it right and if that's what life is like for me, then that's what life is like for other people too.

It's also possible that this vegan crisis of mine has made me more creative in my search for how to do good in the world. It's possible it's made me try just that bit harder than I might have done if I was feeling good and comfortable about myself. It's challenged me to dig deeper.

Quite possibly, the whole thing happened to me so I could write this book and pass on what I've learned to other people struggling with the same issue. I truly hope this has helped you, because although we might have 'failed' in something we really wanted, we can still excel in so many other ways.

Life's too short to be wasting our energy feeling bad about ourselves and frustrated by our limitations and wishing things were different. Life is hard. We don't benefit from making it even harder for ourselves – there's a long line of people who are more than willing to do that for us.

Accept what is, be open to change, do good work. Repeat.

Take the Buddhist approach and restore your own equilibrium first, then share that peace with the rest of the world.

You're okay. You're more than okay. It's crazy how okay you are.

Namaste.

Josephine Moon is a bestselling author of contemporary fiction and non-fiction and is published internationally and in translation. Her first novel, *The Tea Chest*, was shortlisted for an Australian Book Industry Award. She once founded a horse rescue charity, which she ran for three years, is a sponsor for Story Dogs and The Smith Family, ran the 2018 'Authors for Farmers' drought appeal and the 2019 'Authors for Townsville' flood appeal. She lives in the Noosa hinterland on acreage with her husband, son and a tribe of animals that, despite her best intentions, seems to expand every year. She keeps trying to grow vegetables but they almost always succumb to the enthusiastic consumption of a goat or a horse.